by John McPhee

THE PINE BARRENS

THE PINE

BARRENS

JOHN McPHEE

Farrar, Straus and Giroux
New York

Farrar, Straus and Giroux
19 Union Square West, New York 10003

Copyright © 1967, 1968 by John McPhee
All rights reserved
Distributed in Canada by Douglas & McIntyre Ltd.
Printed in the United States of America
Published in 1968 by Farrar, Straus and Giroux
First paperback edition, 1988

The contents of this book originally appeared in
The New Yorker and were developed with the editorial
counsel of William Shawn and Robert Bingham.

The drawings by James Graves on the title page and
on page 85 appeared originally in The New Yorker;
copyright © 1967 by The New Yorker Magazine.

Typography by Guy Fleming

www.fsgbooks.com

38 39 40 41 42 43 44 45

For Pryde
and for her father
Charles Mitchell Brown

CONTENTS

DRAWINGS BY JAMES GRAVES

THE PINE BARRENS

1

The Woods from Hog Wallow

From the fire tower on Bear Swamp Hill, in Washington Township, Burlington County, New Jersey, the view usually extends about twelve miles. To the north, forest land reaches to the horizon. The trees are mainly oaks and pines, and the pines predominate. Occasionally, there are long, dark, serrated stands of Atlantic white cedars, so tall and so closely set that they seem to be spread against the sky on the ridges of hills, when in fact they grow along streams that flow through the forest. To the east, the view is similar, and few people who are not native to the region can discern essential differences from the high cabin of the fire tower, even though one difference is that huge areas out in this direction are covered with dwarf forests, where a man can stand among the trees and see for miles over their uppermost branches. To the south, the view is twice broken slightly—by a lake and by a cranberry bog—but otherwise it, too, goes to the horizon in forest. To the west, pines, oaks, and cedars continue all the way, and the western horizon includes the summit of another hill—Apple

Pie Hill—and the outline of another fire tower, from which the view three hundred and sixty degrees around is virtually the same as the view from Bear Swamp Hill, where, in a moment's sweeping glance, a person can see hundreds of square miles of wilderness. The picture of New Jersey that most people hold in their minds is so different from this one that, considered beside it, the Pine Barrens, as they are called, become as incongruous as they are beautiful. West and north of the Pine Barrens is New Jersey's central transportation corridor, where traffic of freight and people is more concentrated than it is anywhere else in the world. The corridor is one great compression of industrial shapes, industrial sounds, industrial air, and thousands and thousands of houses webbing over the spaces between the factories. Railroads and magnificent highways traverse this crowded scene, and by 1985 New Jersey hopes to have added so many additional high-speed roads that the present New Jersey Turnpike will be quite closely neighbored by the equivalent of at least six other turnpikes, all going in the same direction. In and around the New Jersey corridor, towns indistinguishably abut one another. Of the great unbroken city that will one day reach at least from Boston to Richmond, this section is already built. New Jersey has nearly a thousand people per square mile—the greatest population density of any state in the Union. In parts of northern New Jersey, there are as many as forty thousand people per square mile. In the central area of the Pine Barrens— the forest land that is still so undeveloped that it can be called wilderness—there are only fifteen people per square

§ 4 §

mile. This area, which includes about six hundred and fifty thousand acres, is nearly as large as Yosemite National Park. It is almost identical in size with Grand Canyon National Park, and it is much larger than Sequoia National Park, Great Smoky Mountains National Park, or, for that matter, most of the national parks in the United States. The people who live in the Pine Barrens are concentrated mainly in small forest towns, so the region's uninhabited sections are quite large—twenty thousand acres here, thirty thousand acres there—and in one section of well over a hundred thousand acres there are only twenty-one people. The Pine Barrens are so close to New York that on a very clear night a bright light in the pines would be visible from the Empire State Building. A line ruled on a map from Boston to Richmond goes straight through the middle of the Pine Barrens. The halfway point between Boston and Richmond—the geographical epicenter of the developing megalopolis—is in the northern part of the woods, about twenty miles from Bear Swamp Hill.

Technically, the Pine Barrens are much larger than the thousand or so square miles of them that remain wild, and their original outline is formed by the boundaries of a thick layer of sand soils that covers much of central and southern New Jersey—down the coast from the outskirts of Asbury Park to the Cape May Peninsula, and inland more than halfway across the state. Settlers in the seventeenth and eighteenth centuries found these soils unpromising for farms, left the land uncleared, and began to refer to the region as the Pine Barrens. People in New

Jersey still use the term, with variants such as "the pine belt," "the pinelands," and, most frequently, "the pines." Gradually, development of one kind or another has moved in over the edges of the forest, reducing the circumference of the wild land and creating a man-made boundary in place of the natural one. This transition line is often so abrupt that in many places on the periphery of the pines it is possible to be at one moment in farm-land, or even in a residential development or an industrial zone, and in the next moment to be in the silence of a bewildering green country, where a journey of forty or fifty miles is necessary to get to the farms and factories on the other side. I don't know where the exact center of the pines may be, but in recent years I have spent con-siderable time there and have made outlines of the inte-gral woodland on topographic maps and road maps, and from them I would judge that the heart of the pine coun-try is in or near a place called Hog Wallow. There are twenty-five people in Hog Wallow. Some of them de-scribe it, without any apparent intention to be clever, as a suburb of Jenkins, a town three miles away, which has forty-five people. One resident of Hog Wallow is Fred-erick Chambers Brown. I met him one summer morning when I stopped at his house to ask for water.

Fred Brown's house is on an unpaved road that curves along the edge of a wide cranberry bog. What attracted me to it was the pump that stands in his yard. It was something of a wonder that I noticed the pump, because there were, among other things, eight automobiles in the yard, two of them on their sides and one of them upside down, all ten years old or older. Around the cars were old refrigerators, vacuum cleaners, partly dismantled radios, cathode-ray tubes, a short wooden ski, a large wooden mallet, dozens of cranberry picker's boxes, many tires, an orange crate dated 1946, a cord or so of firewood, mandolins, engine heads, and maybe a thousand other things. The house itself, two stories high, was covered with tarpaper that was peeling away in some places, revealing its original shingles, made of Atlantic white cedar from the stream courses of the surrounding forest. I called out to ask if anyone was home, and a voice inside called back, "Come in. Come in. Come on the hell in."

I walked through a vestibule that had a dirt floor, stepped up into a kitchen, and went on into another room that had several overstuffed chairs in it and a porcelain-topped table, where Fred Brown was seated, eating a pork chop. He was dressed in a white sleeveless shirt, ankle-top shoes, and undershorts. He gave me a cheerful greeting and, without asking why I had come or what I wanted, picked up a pair of khaki trousers that had been tossed onto one of the overstuffed chairs and asked me to sit down. He set the trousers on another chair, and he apologized for being in the middle of his breakfast, explaining that he seldom drank much but the night before he had had a few drinks and this had caused his day to start slowly. "I don't know what's the matter with me, but there's got to be something the matter with me, because drink don't agree with me anymore," he said. He had a raw onion in one hand, and while he talked he shaved slices from the onion and ate them between bites of the chop. He was a muscular and well-built man, with short, bristly white hair, and he had bright, fast-moving eyes in a wide-open face. His legs were trim and strong, with large muscles in the calves. I guessed that he was about sixty, and for a man of sixty he seemed to be in remarkably good shape. He was actually seventy-nine. "My rule is: Never eat except when you're hungry," he said, and he ate another slice of the onion.

In a straight-backed chair near the doorway to the kitchen sat a young man with long black hair, who wore a visored red leather cap that had darkened with age. His shirt was coarse-woven and had eyelets down a V neck that was laced with a thong. His trousers were made of canvas, and he was wearing gum boots. His arms were folded, his legs were stretched out, he had one ankle over the other, and as he sat there he appeared to be sighting carefully past his feet, as if his toes were the outer frame of a gunsight and he could see some sort of target in the floor. When I had entered, I had said hello to him, and he had nodded without looking up. He had a long, straight nose and high cheekbones, in a deeply tanned face that was, somehow, gaunt. I had no idea whether he was shy or hostile. Eventually, when I came to know him, I found him to be as shy a person as I have ever had a chance to know. His name is Bill Wasovwich, and he lives alone in a cabin about half a mile from Fred. First his father, then his mother left him when he was a young boy, and he grew up depending on the help of various people in the pines. One of them, a cranberry grower, employs him and has given him some acreage, in which Bill is building a small cranberry bog of his own, "turfing it out" by hand. When he is not working in the bogs, he goes roaming, as he puts it, setting out cross-country on long, looping journeys, hiking about thirty miles in a typical day, in search of what he calls "events" —surprising a buck, or a gray fox, or perhaps a poacher or a man with a still. Almost no one who is not native to the pines could do this, for the woods have an undulating sameness, and the understory—huckleberries, sheep laurel, sweet fern, high-bush blueberry—is often so dense that a wanderer can walk in a fairly tight circle and think that he is moving in a straight line. State forest rangers spend a good part of their time finding hikers and hunters, some of whom have vanished for days. In his long, pathless journeys, Bill always emerges from the woods near his cabin—and about when he plans to. In the fall, when thousands of hunters come into the pines, he sometimes works as a guide. In the evenings, or in the daytime when he is not working or roaming, he goes to Fred Brown's house and sits there for hours. The old man is a widower whose seven children are long since gone from Hog Wallow, and he is as expansively talkative and worldly as the young one is withdrawn and wild. Although there are fifty-three years between their ages, it is obviously fortunate for each of them to be the other's neighbor.

That first morning, while Bill went on looking at his outstretched toes, Fred got up from the table, put on his pants, and said he was going to cook me a pork chop, because I looked hungry and ought to eat something. It was about noon, and I was even hungrier than I may have looked, so I gratefully accepted his offer, which was a considerable one. There are two or three small general stores in the pines, but for anything as fragile as a fresh pork chop it is necessary to make a round trip from Fred's place of about fifty miles. Fred went into the kitchen and dropped a chop into a frying pan that was crackling with hot grease. He has a fairly new four-burner stove that uses bottled gas. He keeps water in a large bowl on a table in the kitchen and ladles some when he wants it. While he cooked the meat, he looked out a window through a stand of pitch pines and into the cranberry bog. "I saw a big buck out here last night with velvet on his horns," he said. "Them horns is soft when they're in velvet." On a nail high on one wall of the room that Bill and I were sitting in was a large meat cleaver. Next to it was a billy club. The wall itself was papered in a flower pattern, and the wallpaper continued out across the ceiling and down the three other walls, lending the room something of the appearance of the inside of a gift box. In some parts of the ceiling, the paper had come loose. "I didn't paper this year," Fred said. "For the last couple months, I've had sinus." The floor was covered with old rugs. They had been put down in random pieces, and in some places as many as six layers were stacked up. In winter, when the temperature approaches zero, the worst cold comes through the floor. The only source of heat in the house is a wood-burning stove in the main room. There were seven calendars on the walls, all current and none with pictures of nudes. Fading into pastel on one wall was a rotogravure photograph of President and Mrs. Eisenhower. A framed poem read:

> God hath not promised
> Sun without rain
> Joy without sorrow
> Peace without pain.

Noticing my interest in all this, Fred reached into a drawer and showed me what appeared to be a postcard. On it was a photograph of a woman, and Fred said with a straight face that she was his present girl, adding that he meets her regularly under a juniper tree on a road farther south in the pines. The woman, whose appearance suggested strongly that she had never been within a great many miles of the Pine Barrens, was wearing nothing at all.

I asked Fred what all those cars were doing in his yard, and he said that one of them was in running condition and the rest were its predecessors. The working vehicle was a 1956 Mercury. Each of the seven others had at one time or another been his best car, and each, in turn, had lain down like a sick animal and had died right there in the yard, unless it had been towed home after a mishap elsewhere in the pines. Fred recited, with affection, the history of each car. Of one old Ford, for example, he said, "I upset that up to Speedwell in the creek." And of an even older car, a station wagon, he said, "I busted that one up in the snow. I met a car on a little hill, and hit the brake, and hit a tree." One of the cars had met its end at a narrow bridge about four miles from Hog Wallow, where Fred had hit a state trooper, head on.

The pork was delicious and almost crisp. Fred gave me a potato with it, and a pitcher of melted grease from the frying pan to pour over the potato. He also handed me a loaf of bread and a dish of margarine, saying, "Here's your bread. You can have one piece or two. Whatever you want."

Fred apologized for not having a phone, after I asked where I would have to go to make a call, later on. He said, "I don't have no phone because I don't have no electric. If I had electric, I would have had a phone in here a long time ago." He uses a kerosene lamp, a propane lamp, and two flashlights.

He asked where I was going, and I said that I had no particular destination, explaining that I was in the pines because I found it hard to believe that so much unbroken forest could still exist so near the big Eastern cities, and I wanted to see it while it was still there. "Is that so?" he said, three times. Like many people in the pines, he often says things three times. "Is that so? Is *that* so?"

I asked him what he thought of a plan that has been developed by Burlington and Ocean Counties to create a supersonic jetport in the pines, connected by a spur of the Garden State Parkway to a new city of two hundred and fifty thousand people, also in the pines.

"They've been talking about that for three years, and they've never give up," Fred said.

"It'd be the end of these woods," Bill said. This was

the first time I heard Bill speak. I had been there for an hour, and he had not said a word. Without looking up, he said again, "It'd be the end of these woods, I can tell you that."

Fred said, "They could build ten jetports around me. I wouldn't give a damn."

"You ain't going to be around very long," Bill said to him. "It would be the end of these woods."

Fred took that as a fact, and not as an insult. "Yes, it would be the end of these woods," he said. "But there'd be people here you could do business with."

Bill said, "There ain't no place like this left in the country, I don't believe—and I travelled around a little bit, too."

Eventually, I made the request I had intended to make when I walked in the door. "Could I have some water?" I said to Fred. "I have a jerry can and I'd like to fill it at the pump."

"Hell, yes," he said. "That isn't my water. That's God's water. That's God's water. That right, Bill?"

"I *guess* so," Bill said, without looking up. "It's good water, I can tell you that."

"That's God's water," Fred said again. "Take all you want."

Outside, on the pump housing, was a bright-blue coffee tin full of priming water. I primed the pump and, before filling the jerry can, cupped my hands and drank. The water of the Pine Barrens is soft and pure, and there is so much of it that, like the forest above it, it is an incongruity in place and time. In the sand under the pines is a natural reservoir of pure water that, in volume, is the equivalent of a lake seventy-five feet deep with a surface of a thousand square miles. If all the impounding reservoirs, storage reservoirs, and distribution reservoirs in the New York City water system were filled to capacity—from Neversink and Schoharie to the Croton basin and Central Park—the Pine Barrens aquifer would still contain thirty times as much water. So little of this water is used that it can be said to be untapped. Its constant temperature is fifty-four degrees, and, in the language of a hydrological report on the Pine Barrens prepared in 1966 for the United States Geological Survey, "it can be expected to be bacterially sterile, odorless, clear; its chemical purity approaches that of uncontaminated rain-water or melted glacier ice."

In the United States as a whole, only about thirty per cent of the rainfall gets into the ground; the rest is lost to surface runoff or to evaporation, transpiration from leaves, and similar interceptors. In the Pine Barrens, fully half of all precipitation makes its way into the great aquifer, for, as the government report put it, "the loose, sandy soil can imbibe as much as six inches of water per hour." The Pine Barrens rank as one of the greatest natural recharging areas in the world. Thus, the City of New York, say, could take all its daily water requirements out of the pines without fear of diminishing the basic supply. New Jersey could sell the Pine Barrens' "annual ground-water discharge"—the part that at the moment is running off into the Atlantic Ocean—for about two hundred million dollars a year. However, New Jersey does not sell a drop, in part because the state has its own future needs to consider. In the eighteen-seventies, Joseph Wharton, the Philadelphia mineralogist and financier for whom the Wharton School of Finance and Commerce of the University of Pennsylvania is named, recognized the enormous potentiality of the Pine Barrens as a source of water for Philadelphia, and between 1876 and 1890 he gradually acquired nearly a hundred thousand contiguous acres of Pine Barrens land. Wharton's plan called for thirty-three shallow reservoirs in the pines, connected by a network of canals to one stupendous reservoir in Camden, from which an aqueduct would go under the Delaware River and into Philadelphia, where the pure waters of New Jersey would emerge from every tap, replacing a water supply that has been described as "dirty, bacterial soup." Wharton's plan was never executed, mainly because the New Jersey legislature drew itself together and passed prohibiting legislation. Wharton died in 1909. The Wharton Tract, as his immense New Jersey landholding was called, has remained undeveloped. It was considered as a site for the United States Air Force Academy. The state was slow in acquiring it in the public interest, but at last did so in 1955, and the whole of it is now Wharton State Forest.

All the major river systems in the United States are polluted, and so are most of the minor ones, but all the small rivers and streams in the Pine Barrens are potable.

The pinelands have their own divide. The Pine Barrens rivers rise in the pines. Some flow west to the Delaware; most flow southeast directly into the sea. There are no through-flowing streams in the pines—no waters coming in from cities and towns on higher ground, as is the case almost everywhere else on the Atlantic coastal plain. I have spent many weekends on canoe trips in the Pine Barrens—on the Wading River, the Oswego, the Batsto, the Mullica. There is no white water in any of these rivers, but they move along fairly rapidly; they are so tortuous that every hundred yards or so brings a new scene—often one that is reminiscent of canoeing country in the northern states and in Canada. Even on bright days, the rivers can be dark and almost sunless under stands of white cedar, and then, all in a moment, they run into brilliant sunshine where the banks rise higher and the forest of oak and pine is less dense. One indication of the size of the water resource below the Pine Barrens is that the streams keep flowing without great declines in volume even in prolonged times of drought. When streams in other parts of New Jersey were reduced to near or total dryness in recent years, the rivers in the pines were virtually unaffected. The characteristic color of the water in the streams is the color of tea—a phenomenon, often called "cedar water," that is familiar in the Adirondacks, as in many other places where tannins and other organic waste from riparian cedar trees combine with iron from the ground water to give the rivers a deep color. In summer, the cedar water is ordinarily so dark that the riverbeds are obscured, and while drifting along one has a feeling of being afloat on a river of fast-moving potable ink. For a few days after a long rain, however, the water is almost colorless. At these times, one can look down into it from a canoe and see the white sand bottom, ten or twelve feet below, and it is as clear as an image in the lens of a camera, with sunken timbers now and again coming into view and receding rapidly, at the speed of the river. Every strand of subsurface grass and every contour of the bottom sand is so sharply defined that the deep water above it seems, and is, irresistibly pure. Sea captains once took the cedar water of the Pine Barrens rivers with them on voyages, because cedar water would remain sweet and potable longer than any other water they could find.

According to the government report, "The Pine Barrens have no equal in the northeastern United States not only for magnitude of water in storage and availability of recharge, but also for the ease and economy with which a large volume of water could be withdrawn." Typically, a pipe less than two inches in diameter driven thirty feet into the ground will produce fifty-five gallons a minute, and a twelve-inch pipe could bring up a million gallons a day. But, with all this, the vulnerability of the Pine Barrens aquifer is disturbing to contemplate. The water table is shallow in the pines, and the aquifer is extremely sensitive to contamination. The sand soil, which is so superior as a catcher of rain, is not good at filtering out or immobilizing wastes. Pollutants, if they happen to get into the water, can travel long distances. Industry or even extensive residential development in the central pinelands could spread contaminants widely through the underground reservoir.

When I had finished filling the jerry can from Fred Brown's pump, I took another drink, and I said to him, "You're lucky to live over such good water."

"You're telling me," he said. "You can put this water in a jug and put it away for a year and it will still be the same. Water from outside of these woods would stink. Outside of these woods, some water stinks when you pump it out of the ground. The people that has dug deep around here claims that there are streams of water under this earth that runs all the time."

In the weeks that followed, I stopped in many times to see Fred, and saw nearly as much of Bill. They rode with me through the woods, in my car, for five and six hours at a time. In the evenings, we returned to Fred's place with food from some peripheral town. It is possible to cross the pines on half a dozen state or federal roads, but very little of interest is visible from them. Several county roads—old crown roads with uneven macadam surfaces —connect the pine communities, but it is necessary to get off the paved roads altogether in order to see much of the forest. The areas are spacious—fifty, sixty, and seventy-five thousand acres—through which run no paved roads of any kind. There are many hundreds of miles of un-paved roads through the pines—two tracks in the sand, with underbrush growing up between them. Hunters use them, and foresters, firefighters, and woodcutters. A number of these sand roads have been there, and have remained unchanged, since before the American Revolution. They developed, for the most part, as Colonial stage routes, trails to charcoal pits, pulpwood-and-lumber roads, and connecting roads between communities that have disappeared from the world. In a place called Washington, five of these roads converge in the forest, as if from star points, and they suggest the former importance of Washington, but all that is left of the town is a single fragment of a stone structure. The sand roads are marked on topographic maps with parallel dotted lines, and driving on them can be something of a sport. It is possible to drive all day on the sand roads, and more than halfway across the state, but most people need to stop fairly often to study the topographic maps, for the roads sometimes come together in fantastic ganglia, and even when they are straight and apparently uncomplicated they constantly fork, presenting unclear choices between the main chance and culs-de-sac, of which there are many hundreds. No matter where we were—far up near Mt. Misery, in the northern part of the pines, or over in the western extremities of the Wharton Tract, or down in the southeast, near the Bass River—Fred kept calling out directions. He always knew exactly where he was going. Fred was nearly forty when the first paved roads were built in the pines. Once, not far from the Godfrey Bridge on the Wading River, he said, "Look at these big pines. You would never think that I was as old as these big pines, would you? I seen all of these big pines grow. I remember this when it was all cut down for charcoal." A short distance away, he pointed into a high stand of pitch pines and scarlet oaks, and he said, "That's the old Joe Holloway field. Holloway had a water-powered sawmill." In another part of the woods, we passed a small bald area, and he said, "That's the Dan Dillett field, where Dan made charcoal." As the car kept moving, bouncing in the undulations of the sand and scraping against blueberry bushes and scrub-oak boughs, Fred kept narrating, picking fragments of the past out of the forest, in moments separated by miles: "Right here in this piece of woods is more rattlesnakes than anyplace else in the State of New Jersey. They had a sawmill in there. They used to kill three or four rattlesnakes when they was watering their horses at noon. Rattlesnakes like water. . . . See that fire tower over there? The man in that tower—you take him fifty yards away from that tower and he's lost. He don't know the woods. He don't know the woods. He don't know the woods. He don't know nothing. He can't even fry a hamburger. . . . I've gunned this part of the woods since I was ten years old. I know every foot of it here. . . . Apple Pie Hill is a thunderstriking high hill. You don't realize how high until you get up here. It's the long slope of a hill that makes a high one. . . . See that open spot in there? A group of girls used to keep a house in there. It was called Noah's Ark. . . . I worked this piece of cedar off here. . . . I worked this bog for Joe Wharton once. My father used to work for Joe Wharton, too. He used to come and stay with my father. Joe Wharton was the nicest man you ever seen. That is, if you didn't lie to him. He was quiet. He didn't smile very often. I don't know as I ever heard him laugh out loud. . . . These are the Hocken Lowlands." The Hocken Lowlands surround the headwaters of Tulpehocken Creek, about five miles northwest of Hog Wallow, and are not identified on maps, not even on the large-scale topographic maps. As we moved along, Fred had a name for almost every rise and dip in the land. "This is Sandy Ridge," he said. "That road once went in to a bog. Houses were there. Now there's nothing there. . . . This is Bony's Hole. A man named Bony used to water his horse here." Every so often, Fred would reach into his pocket and touch up his day with a minimal sip from a half pint of whiskey. He merely touched the bottle to his lips, then put it away. He did this at irregular intervals, and one day, when he had a new half pint, he took more than five hours to reduce the level of the whiskey from the neck to the shoulders of the bottle. At an intersection of two sand roads in the Wharton Tract, he pointed to a depression in the ground and said, "That hole in the ground was the cellar of an old jug tavern. That cellar was where they kept the jugs. There was a town here called Mount. That tavern is where my grandpop got drunk the last time he got drunk in his life. Grandmother went up to get him. When she came in, he said, 'Mary, what are you doing here?' He was so ashamed to see her there—and his daughter with her. He left a jug of whiskey right on the table, and his wife took one of his hands and his daughter the other and they led him out of there and past Washington

Field and home to Jenkins Neck. He lived fifty years. He lived fifty years, and growed cranberries. He lived fifty years more, and he was never drunk again."

One evening, when it was almost dark and we were about five miles from Fred's place, he told me to stop, and he said, "See that upland red cedar? I helped set that out." Red cedar is not native in the Pine Barrens, and this one stood alone among the taller oaks and pines, in a part of the forest that seemed particularly remote. "I went to school there, by that red cedar," Fred said. "There was twenty-five of us in the school. We all walked. We wore leather boots in the winter that got soaked through and your feet froze. When you got home, you had to pull off your boots on a bootjack. In the summer, when I was a boy, if you wanted to go anywhere you rolled up your pantlegs, put your shoes on your shoulder, and you walked wherever you was going. The pigs and cows was everywhere. There was wild bulls, wild cows, wild boars. That's how Hog Wallow got its name. They call them the good old days. What do you think of that, Bill?"

"I wish I was back there, I can tell you that," Bill said.

2

The Vanished Towns

DRIVING ALONG A SAND ROAD BETWEEN the vanished town of Calico and the vanished town of Munion Field, we passed a house that was so many miles from any other house that Fred said, with evident admiration, "He got well in away from everybody, didn't he? He got well in away from everybody." Fred made a similar remark every time we passed a house or cabin that was particularly deep and alone in the woods. Getting—or staying—away from everybody is a criterion that apparently continues to mean as much to many of the people in the pines as it did to some of their forebears who first settled there. Tories, for example, fled into the pines during the American Revolution. People with names like Britton and Brower, loyal to the King, and sometimes covered with feathers and tar, left their homes in Colonial cities and took refuge in the Pine Barrens. Also during the eighteenth century, when the farmlands of western New Jersey were heavily populated with Quakers, the Pine Barrens served as a catch basin for Quakers who could not live up to the standards of the

Quaker code. A Quaker named Ridgway, for example, brought before a Quaker grand jury in west Jersey and found guilty of working on the Sabbath, was exiled to the pines, where Ridgways live in numbers today. Many young Quakers "went against the testimony" by fighting in the Revolutionary War, and when they came home after Yorktown they found that they were no longer welcome, so they built themselves cabins in the pines. Sooy is a German name more common in the pines than Smith. After the British defeats at Trenton and Princeton, Hessian soldiers deserted the British Army in considerable numbers, and some of them went into the Pine Barrens. Of all the stories of the origins of people in the pines, the one of the Hessian soldiers seems to have achieved the largest circulation elsewhere in New Jersey. Some New Jersey people who do not live in the Pine Barrens assume that everyone in the woods is a Hessian descendant, and the term "Hessians" is often used in reference to all the people of the region. French Huguenots first settled Mt. Misery (Miséricorde), and Huguenot names, such as Bozarth, remain in the Pine Barrens. Some Negroes fled from slavery into the pines, but the Negro population there has always been close to nil. A Negro named James Still, who was born in the Pine Barrens in 1812, educated himself in medical botany, became known as the Doctor of the Pines, and eventually wrote an autobiography, which was published by J. B. Lippincott in 1877. Dr. Still treated piles with sassafras roots, and he made a "cough balsam" using the roots of spikenard and skunk cabbage. He treated hypochondria, on the other hand, with wit and wisdom, and thereby effected "cures" where many physicians failed. Of one such case, in which he had been called in to replace another doctor, Still wrote, "The doctor treated the case in a scientific manner, without success. I treated it according to the laws of nature." Among medical men in south-central New Jersey, Still was known as Black Jim. American Indians had almost no interest in the pinelands when the whole of the country was theirs, but in the seventeen-fifties they, too, sought asylum in the woods. At an interracial conference that followed a massacre in west Jersey, the tribesmen asked for land they could call their own, and they were given 3,258 acres in the Pine Barrens, where there had never been an Indian settlement of any size or duration. The place was called Brotherton, and was the first Indian reservation in North America. The Indians tried to make it work. They dammed a stream and set up a sawmill and a gristmill, but disease and poverty were the main results of the experiment, and in 1802 most of the Indians went off to northern New York and eventually to Indian Territory. Numerous people in the Pine Barrens today are descended, in part, from Indians who remained. A few are full-blooded, or something close to it. George Crummel, a charcoal-maker who lived in Jenkins Neck and died there in 1964, was the great-grandson of Isaac Cromo, a chief of the Leni Lenape. On the site of the Brotherton reservation is a hamlet called Indian Mills.

The Pine Barrens have been something besides a place of retreat, however. Isolation was not the goal of most of the early Englishmen, Welshmen, and Scots, who arrived, in large part, via New England, and whose names remain—Applegate, Wescoat, Jenkins, Brown, Cranmer (now Crammer or Cramer as well as Cranmer, a prodigious family that traces itself to Thomas Cranmer, the Archbishop of Canterbury), Bartlett, Leek, Leeds, Southwick, Wainwright. One thing that attracted people to the pines was good money in smuggling—a respectable business in Colonial America. The Pine Barrens were a smuggler's El Dorado, for all that wilderness so close to New York and Philadelphia was extraordinary even two hundred years ago, and through the inlets from the sea up the Pine Barrens rivers went hundreds of thousands of tons of sugar, molasses, tea, and coffee, while ships of the Royal Navy patrolled the roadsteads of Boston, New York, and Philadelphia. Cargoes were transferred to wagons and sent inland over the sand roads, often moving by night. One of the earliest of the merchant smugglers was John Mathis, whose contemporaries always called him Great John. His descendants are spread across the pine belt today. He sent lumber from the Pine Barrens to islands in the Caribbean, and when the ships came back he smuggled in his fortune in rum.

There was also iron in the pinelands. Most of the now vanished towns in the pines were iron towns—small, precursive Pittsburghs, in every part of the forest, where fine grades of pig and wrought iron were made. One of the geological curiosities of the Pine Barrens is that rainwater soaking down through fallen pine needles and other forest litter takes on enough acid to leach out iron from the sands below; the dissolved iron moves underground into the streams, where it oxidizes on contact with the air and forms a patch of scum on the surface that is partly rust brown and partly iridescent blue, and resembles an oil slick left by an outboard motor; drifting over to the edges of the streams, this iron-oxide film permeates the sands and gravels of the riverbanks and cements them together into a sandstone composite that has been known for centuries as bog iron. From it ironmasters of the Pine Barrens made cannonballs by the thousand and sent them by wagon over the sand roads and on to the Continental Army at Valley Forge and elsewhere. They brought in seashells for flux, and used charcoal from the pinewoods to fire their forges and furnaces. They made cannon as well as shot, and they ordnanced the War of 1812 as well as the American Revolution. The twenty-four-pounders with which Stephen Decatur armed his flagship when he took his Marines to Algiers, Tunisia, and Tripoli were cast at Hanover Furnace, in the Pine Barrens, in 1814, and Decatur himself was there to supervise the casting and to test the product. Forty-five years later, an unsigned article in the May, 1859, *Atlantic* described the scene when the new guns came out of their molds: "Decatur ordered each one to be loaded with repeated charges of powder and ball, and pointed into the woods. Then, for miles between the grazed and quivering boles, crashed the missiles of destruction, startling bear and deer and squirrel and raccoon, and leaving traces of their passage which are even still occasionally discovered." Ironworkers in the pines made the steam cylinder for one of John Fitch's experimental steamboats, and they made the wrought-iron fence that once surrounded Independence Hall. They made nails, firebacks, sugar-mill gudgeons, Dutch ovens, and kettles that could hold as much as a hundred and twenty-five gallons. Bog iron is remarkably reluctant to rust. In some graveyards in the Pine Barrens, there are iron tombstones, and around old houses are walks made of iron flagstones. Iron stoves that bear the town name Atsion over their fuelling doors were made in a community that had a population of seven hundred in the early nineteenth century and has a population of fifteen today. A schooner named Atsion, loaded with stoves, made regular runs down the Mullica River and up the coast to New York and on to Albany. Atsion Forge was at one time owned by Samuel Richards, who built a glorious mansion in Atsion. The mansion is still there, off Route 206, in the Wharton Tract. It has iron windowsills. Atsion Forge had been established in 1765 by a man named Charles Read, who also built a furnace at Batsto, about ten miles away. In 1770, a Philadelphian named John Cox bought Batsto for twenty-three hundred and fifty pounds. Cox was a member of the first Committee of Correspondence and a member of the Council of Safety. With the coming of war, he became a lieutenant colonel and, eventually, assistant quartermaster general of the Continental Armies. His ironworks at Batsto flourished on war contracts from the Quartermaster Corps. In 1778, Cox sold Batsto for forty thousand pounds—a capital gain of about sixteen hundred per cent. The deal was exquisitely complicated, involving a number of new owners, among them Nathanael Greene, the quartermaster general under whom Cox served, and Charles Pettit, another assistant quartermaster general. Cox, furthermore, arranged to repurchase a one-twelfth share in Batsto for himself. Batsto was to reach its most developed stage in the eighteen-thirties and eighteen-forties, when the town had a population of eight hundred. Batsto, like Atsion, is one of the few iron towns that remain in the Pine Barrens. The headquarters of the Wharton State Forest is there, and the town, which was purchased in its entirety by Joseph Wharton in 1876, spreads out around the Batsto manor house much as it did a hundred years ago. The state has restored its water-powered sawmill, and sawyers cut white cedar there and make cedar shingles for use in restoration of Batsto buildings. Batsto is a functioning relic. In its gristmill, the great stones grind corn, and the miller sells cornmeal to the public.

The furnaces of the Pine Barrens were started up each year in the spring when the ice was gone and spillways from dammed streams again turned the waterwheels that powered giant bellows, which kept the furnaces in blast until winter froze them out. Men worked in twelve-hour shifts. There were no days off, and the happiest day of the year was the day the furnace went out of blast. In the furnace towns, bog iron was crushed under great stamping hammers, and in the forge towns pig iron was worked into anconies of wrought iron under forge hammers that weighed more than five hundred pounds. Miles away, teamsters coming over the sand roads with loads of shells from the coast could hear the din through the forest, as could ore raisers out in the bogs, and colliers—as charcoal-makers were known in the pines—working at their pits. Caleb Earle, company clerk in a furnace town called Martha, kept a semi-official diary from March 31, 1808, to April 27, 1815. It is terse and sporadic, averaging about sixty-five short entries a year, but it is the only contemporary record of life in a Pine Barrens town. Martha Furnace was built in 1793, a few miles southeast of Jenkins. The furnace has long since collapsed, and a large earth-covered mound remains where a high double-walled pyramid of bricks once stood. The spillway runs back to a broken dam on the Oswego River at Martha Pond. There were about fifty houses in the town, a central mansion, a school, and a small hospital—all interspersed with stands of catalpa trees, which were planted throughout the town and are about all that remains of it. With the exception of the furnace mound, there is not a trace of a structure in Martha now. The streets are bestrewn with green and blue glittering slag, but they are indistinguishable from the sand roads that come through the woods from several directions to the town, and if it were not for the old and weirdly leaning catalpa trees, it would be possible to pass through Martha without sensing its difference from the surrounding woodland.

January 4, 1809—Frost stopped furnace wheel several times.

January 7, 1809—Ore teams hauled hay. Blew the furnace out at eight o-clock p.m. All hands drunk.

§ 30 §

April 20, 1809—At twenty-five minutes past two o-clock p.m., put the furnace in blast. Delaney and Cox fillers. Hedger putting in the ore. Donaghau banksman.

Some of the ironworkers were indentured servants, and some of these had been English criminals. Most were not indentured. Each man's specialty fitted in somewhere on a scale of status, with colliers at the low end, founders at the top, and, somewhere between, blacksmiths, pattern-makers, and molders.

July 28, 1809—Molders all agreed to quit work and went to the beach.

July 30, 1809—Molders returned from the beach. J. Ventling drunk and eating eggs at the slitting mill. Josh Townsend wanting to fight J. Williamson. Furnace boiled and the metal consolidated in the gutter.

July 31, 1809—Molders all idle.

August 1, 1809—This month begins with good weather. Molders commenced molding for the first time since they came from the beach.

In the idiom of the community, a man who quit without giving notice was said to have made a clandestine retreat, and childbirth was spoken of as a muster or a general muster.

January 29, 1809—Terence Toole made a clandestine retreat from the chopping. Left his ax, blankets, etc.

December 6, 1810—The men begin to complain of beef. They want pork.

December 21, 1810—Rain. Furnace made very bad iron owing to the wet weather.

May 27, 1811—Cross carting logs for ore cabin. Mary Griffith made a muster.

July 4, 1811—Independence. May the name of Washington be immortal and the federal constitution may it never fail.

July 10, 1811—Mary Luker made a general muster and brought forth a daughter.

July 27, 1811—William Rose and his father both drunk and lying on the crossway.

February 18, 1812—Teams carting ore from Sassafras. Jane Hamilton conceived and brought forth a son. Women are all very fruitful, multiply, and replenish.

August 17, 1812—Molders a deer hunting. George Townsend shot one but did not get it. Mr. Evans surveying. Furnace making bad iron.

September 17, 1812—Jane Hamilton was this day tried by the synod of her church. The crime alleged against her was for using spiritual liquor, but acquitted.

October 13, 1812—Election at Bodine's. Hands chiefly there. Some very drunk.

October 30, 1812—Molders out a hunting. J. Townsend killed a deer.

December 16, 1812—Sarah Taylor brought down a load of cheese. William Rose died very sudden in the coaling, supposed drunk.

April 12, 1813—William Mick's widow arrived here in pursuit of J. Mick, who she says has knocked her up.

June 2, 1813—Great conflagration. The furnace and warehouse was this day entirely consumed, but fortunately no lives lost. John Craig got very much burnt.

August 23, 1814—Has a great fire in the pines.

November 14, 1814—The dam broke this morning.

All the ore-raisers at work at it.

February 24, 1815—This day we had news of peace confirmed. Teams all standing still. Snowing and raining.

Bodine's Tavern, where the men of Martha went to vote on October 13, 1812, was a few miles south of Martha, on the Wading River. The jug taverns of the pines—so called because rare was the traveller who passed by one without going in to top up his liquor jug—were places of assembly for many public events, from elections and town meetings to community suppers and the regular drills of the standing militia. On election days, the suffrage was exercised with abandon. Not only was the bar open, but the local candidates were there, and the winner—as a rule—was the man who stood the greatest number of drinks for the electorate. The voters drank metheglin (mead and water with a zest of herbs), cider royall (highly concentrated cider), mimbo (rum and muscovado sugar), straight rum, whiskey, gin, beer. The same men drank the same drinks when they turned up at the same tavern as militiamen assembling for Training Day, an antecedent of what today would be a National Guard meeting. Training Days tended to mock rather than to improve military skills and procedures. While the tavernkeepers kept making rounds with mimbo and metheglin, drums rolled and fifes put a sense of celebration into the air. Officers, wearing stunning blue American uniforms that were braided in gold and studded with brass, rapped out sharp orders, which no one obeyed. After a little more mimbo, fights began to occur in the ranks. There were casualties. Some men fell as a result of blows received, and many more toppled over without assistance. Nonetheless, it was apparently important that there be some simulacrum of command, for Captain Townsend, of Martha, was summarily court-martialled at Bodine's Tavern on April 1, 1814, a Training Day, for being too drunk to give orders.

Jug taverns were located at most of the important intersections of the sand roads, since the volume of freight and passenger travel was considerable in the eighteenth century and early nineteenth century in the pines. One major route ran from Philadelphia to Tuckerton, a coastal town on the edge of the Pine Barrens and the third officially established port of entry in the United States. The Philadelphia-Tuckerton stage stopped at Long-a-Coming, New Jersey (now Berlin), and then moved east through the pines, to Atsion, Quaker Bridge, Mount, and Washington, and on to the Wading River and eventually to Tuckerton. A large part of this road still exists, can be driven in an automobile, and has not been paved, oiled, or even scraped since it was cut through the woods when New Jersey was a royal colony. In some places between Atsion and Quaker Bridge, the road divides, because the wagon and stagecoach traffic was so heavy that it was necessary to have eastbound and westbound lanes in what may have been the first dual highway in North America. Bodine's Tavern was built where the Tuckerton Road crossed the Wading River. Similarly, a man named Arthur Thompson built Thompson's Tavern at Quaker Bridge, where a group of Quakers had put up a bridge over the Batsto River in 1772 in memory of numerous Quakers who had drowned while attempting to ford the stream. In 1805, four botanists who were staying at Thompson's Tavern went into the woods near Quaker Bridge and—in what proved to be a major botanical discovery—found an odd, small, beautiful fern (*Schizaea pusilla*, the curly grass fern), which grows almost exclusively in the Pine Barrens. Jonathan Cramer ran the tavern at Mount, where Fred Brown's grandfather had his last drink on earth. The tavern in Washington, in some ways the most important one in the pines, was used by the Committee of Safety during the Revolution as recruiting headquarters for the area. When a reasonably young and healthy-looking ironworker came through the door, a recruiting sergeant would clap him on the shoulder, buy him a drink, and attempt to persuade him to fight for his independence.

Weddings were held at Washington Tavern, and to one wedding during the Revolution came an uninvited guest named Joseph Mulliner, who, so the story goes, jabbed a pistol into the groom's ribs and told him to leave, which the groom did. Waving his pistol, Mulliner danced with the bride, and then, after drinking a yard or so of ale, retreated into the night alone. Mulliner, who became a legend in the pines, was the leader of a band of outlaws, and it was said that he recognized the groom as a fellow-outlaw and a deadly personal enemy. In general, Mulliner's biography has been cleaned up by romantic retelling, and it was even converted into fiction by Charles J. Peterson, whose novel *Kate Aylesford*, published in

1855, is set in the Pine Barrens during the Revolution and has for a villain a dashing character modelled on Mulliner, who kidnaps the heroine. Mulliner was actually one of a class of particularly brutal criminals who lived in numbers in the pines during the war and called themselves Pine Refugees. This was meant to suggest that they were Tories, like the Brittons and the Browers, and that they were taking refuge for their own safety, were loyal to the King, and were therefore serving the King when they murdered people committed to the Revolutionary cause. The Refugees, who travelled—frequently masked—in packs on the sand roads, actually killed and robbed as many Tories as Whigs. They were known also as Pine Robbers and Pine Banditti. Posses hunted them down. When a Pine Robber was shot, people assembled to celebrate. Richard Bird, a gang leader like Mulliner, was shot by a posse that had followed him to a cabin in the woods where he was visiting a girl. The shot that killed him was fired through a window, and when the posse went inside they found the girl going through his pockets. The Pine Robbers raped women of almost all ages, they killed clergymen, and they stabbed or shot many people who knelt before them and begged for life. In 1781, Joseph Mulliner was caught, dancing with a girl at another party he had crashed, and he was tried and hanged.

A considerable part of the goods that moved inland over the sand roads during the Revolution had been captured at sea by pirates from the pines who carried letters of marque from the Continental Congress authorizing them to attack, possess, and sell British ships and British cargoes. During the war, up and down the American coast, privateers captured well over a thousand British ships, worth upward of twenty million dollars. New Jersey pirates hauled so many of these ships into the Pine Barrens rivers that British hulls and scattered timbers are still in the riverbeds. There is a dam at Penny Pot, on the Great Egg Harbor River, that was made from salvaged ship timbers. It was built to be nothing more than a cranberry dam, but it has in it seventy-five thousand dollars' worth of teak. One New Jersey sailor went out to sea in a small whaleboat with nine other men and came back into the Mullica River with a British warship and a British brig, which were auctioned, like most of the New Jersey prizes, at The Forks, near Batsto. In 1778, England tried to put down the New Jersey privateers. A flotilla of ships and eight hundred soldiers surprised Chestnut Neck, a fort across the mouth of the Mullica from Tuckerton, and wiped it out. The force then moved upstream, intending to destroy the ships of privateers along the way and ultimately to raze the ironworks at Batsto. But a small boy warned Batsto that the British soldiers were approaching, and before they could do much of anything they were ambushed and their campaign was finished.

The iron industry in the Pine Barrens lasted for about half a century after the Revolution, and, curiously, reached its point of highest development just before it vanished. In the eighteen-thirties, the iron towns were as populous and productive as they would ever be, and other industries that had developed concomitantly were flourishing, too. Woodcutters supplied great amounts of

§ 37 §

cordwood to New York and to Philadelphia, as they had for a hundred years. Sawyers, working mainly with white cedar, made shingles, clapboards, lumber, lath, and shipboards. Cedar panelling from the Pine Barrens had been used since before the Revolution in the homes of the rich of Manhattan. Cabinetmakers kept up the high standards of their predecessor Benjamin Randolph, who lived in Speedwell, just north of Hog Wallow, and owned an iron furnace there. Randolph made the writing desk that Thomas Jefferson used when he wrote the Declaration of Independence, and he also made a wing chair that would be auctioned, in the twentieth century, for thirty-three thousand dollars. The era of iron in the pines ended after high-grade bituminous coal and iron ore were discovered in western Pennsylvania. The ore in western Pennsylvania was superior to the bog iron of New Jersey, not in the quality of the iron inside it but in the economy with which the iron could be got out. Coal had every advantage over charcoal. Iron smelting on a large scale began in Pennsylvania around 1840. Batsto Furnace blew out for the last time in 1848. Martha Furnace and Atsion Forge closed down about then, too. In less than twenty years, no ironworks of any kind were left in the pines. Depletion of the wood supply helped to force the closings. Each furnace used a thousand acres of pine per year, and the trees could not grow rapidly enough to permit an equilibrium. As early as 1846, the colporteur records of the American Tract Society reported, "The wood is generally gone, so the people are poorer than they were a few years ago and are likely to remain poor. Towns and populous neighborhoods can never be, on such barren sand." The pine towns did not give up at once, however. They tried to make other things. For example, the Wading River Forge & Slitting Mill, where pig iron from nearby Martha had been made into nails and other cut products, was converted into a paper mill. Heavy papers were manufactured there from marsh grasses. Some writing paper was produced as well, but it was yellow from the iron in the Wading River, and the line was discontinued. When four brothers named Harris bought the paper mill in 1855, the name of the community around it was changed from McCartyville to Harrisville. The Harrises were fussy but benevolent employers. Each man who worked for them got a rent-free house, a garden, horse-drawn-ambulance service, free ice, and a dollar and twenty-five cents a day for working from six until six. Harrisville was a neat little town, with picket fences, and with gas lamps lining its streets. If Richard Harris, one of the brothers, happened to see a gate ajar, he would look up the resident of the house behind the gate and tell him to try, please, not to be so unkempt. Ultimately, Harrisville could not compete with paper mills in other parts of the country. The ruins of the great paper factory—high, arched stone walls three feet thick —have gradually crumbled, but enough of them remains to suggest the scale of the original structure, which was seven hundred and fifty feet long. Of the town itself and the gas lamps there is nothing. Elsewhere in the Pine Barrens, glass factories were built in an attempt to find an industry that could replace iron. The first mason jar was made in the pines. Herman City, a hamlet in the Pine Barrens today, was given its name by visionary glassmakers who imagined tall buildings rising above the pine trees, financed by fortunes made in glass. Window-panes were manufactured at Batsto, and also panes for gas street lamps, but by 1867 the surrounding forest was so cut over that the glassworks were forced to close for lack of fuel. The walls, before long, fell. Now, a hundred years later, a young archeologist named Budd Wilson has removed the sand and turf from the remains of the Batsto glass factories, no trace of which was above the surface. The project has the appearance of a dig on an island in the Aegean. Wilson has revealed the floors of the factories and the intricate brickwork, still intact, of the bases of glassmaking ovens. Perhaps on these foundations, or perhaps on replica foundations nearby, Wilson hopes to have glass factories again in operation in Batsto soon, as a part of the general restoration of the town.

3

The Separate World

In 1859, WHEN THE POPULATION OF THE central Pine Barrens was about as large as it has ever been, the area had nonetheless remained wild enough for the *Atlantic* to report, "It is a region aboriginal in savagery, grand in the aspects of untrammelled Nature; where forests extend in uninterrupted lines over scores of miles; where we may wander a good day's journey without meeting half-a-dozen human faces; where stately deer will bound across our path, and bears dispute our passage through the cedar-brakes; where, in a word, we may enjoy the undiluted essence, the perfect wildness, of woodland life." The magazine feared, however, that accelerated development would soon clear this wild country. "It is scarcely too much to anticipate that, within five years, thousands of acres, now dense with pines and cedars of a hundred rings, will be laid out in blooming market-gardens and in fields of generous corn," the article concluded. "Five years hence, bears and deer will be a tradition, panthers and raccoons a myth, partridges and quails a vain and melancholy recollection, in what shall

§ 41 §

then be known as what was once the pines." The trend
the *Atlantic* anticipated was the reverse of the one that
actually took place. As the last of the iron furnaces gradually blew out and the substitute industries failed, people
either left the pines or began to lead self-sufficient back-
woods lives, and while the rest of the State of New Jersey developed toward its twentieth-century aspect, the
Pine Barrens all but returned to their pre-Colonial deso-
lation, becoming, as they have remained, a distinct and
separate world. The people of the pines came to be
known as pineys—a term that is as current today as it
was at the turn of the century. After a generation or two
had lived in isolation, the pineys began to fear people
from the outside, and travellers often reported that when
they approached a cabin in the pines the people scattered
and hid behind trees. This was interpreted, by some, as
a mark of lunacy. It was simply fear of the unknown.

The pineys had little fear of their surroundings, from
which they drew an adequate living. A yearly cycle
evolved that is still practiced, but by no means univer-
sally, as it once was. With the first warmth of spring,
pineys took their drags—devices with tines, something
like hand cultivators—and went into the lowland forests
to gather sphagnum moss. This extraordinary material
has such a capacity for absorbing water that one can
squeeze it and twist it and wring it a dozen times and
water will still come pouring out. Since the water is
acidulous and somewhat antiseptic, sphagnum moss was
used by soldiers during the Revolution when they lacked
ordinary bandages. Florists provided a large part of the

market for the pineys' moss. Boxes of cut flowers sent out by florists' shops all over the East used to contain—under and around the flowers—protective beds of sphagnum from the pines. Plastic moss has largely replaced sphagnum moss in the floral trade, but a market remains for it, and some people still gather it.

In June and July, when the wild blueberries of the Pine Barrens ripened on the bush, the pineys hung large homemade baskets around their necks, bent the blueberry bushes over the baskets, and beat the stems with short clubs. The berries, if just ripe enough, rained into the baskets. Fred Brown told me one day that he had knocked off his share of "huckleberries" in his time, and that many people still go out after them every summer. In the vernacular of the pines, huckleberries are blueberries, wild or cultivated. Huckleberries are also huckleberries, and this confuses outsiders but not pineys. Fred explained to me, when I pressed him, that "hog huckleberries" are huckleberries and "sugar huckleberries" are blueberries. He said, "Ain't nothing for a man to go out and knock off two hundred pounds in less than a day." In 1967, the average price for wild blueberries was fourteen cents a pound. People who gather wild blueberries now use No. 2 galvanized tubs instead of baskets. They beat the bushes with lengths of rubber hose. "Wild berries got a better taste than cultivated berries," Fred said. "Mrs. Wagner's Pies won't make pies with just cultivated berries." Millions of blueberry bushes grow wild in the pines, but when a forester who was doing field work for a doctoral thesis recently asked a piney assistant to cut one down, the piney refused.

Cranberries followed blueberries in the cycle of the pines. Cranberries grow wild along the streams and are white in the summer and red in the fall. In the eighteen-sixties and eighteen-seventies, people began to transplant them to the cleared and excavated bogs where ore raisers had removed bog iron, and that was the beginning of commercial cranberry growing in the Pine Barrens, where about a third of the United States total is now grown. Cranberry bogs are shallow basins, dammed on all sides, so that streams can fill them in late autumn and keep cold winter winds from drying out the vines. The older bogs were turfed out by hand, and the dams were built from the turf. In the fall, the berries were harvested by hand, with many-tined wooden scoops that went through the vines like large claws. Cranberry scoops are so primitive in appearance that they are sold as antiques in shops on Third Avenue and in Bucks County. In a few bogs in the Pine Barrens, scoops are still used, and only five years ago all bogs used them.

In winter, the cycle moved on to cordwood and charcoal. Woodcutters, in the seventeenth century, were among the first people in the pines. They were needed in the iron era, they remained when it was over, and they are still there. They are getting a good price for their pulpwood—seven dollars a cord. With a chain saw, a man can cut a cord of pine in less than an hour. "Oak isn't worth nothing, but the pine is way up," Fred Brown said one day. Charcoal burning also continued beyond the iron era and was actually a major occupation in the Pine Barrens until the Second World War. In the eighteen-fifties, fifty schooners made regular runs with charcoal from the Pine Barrens to New York. Countless four-mule teams hauled charcoal over the sand roads to Philadelphia in covered wagons. Eight-mule teams hauled larger wagons, full of the best grade, to the Philadelphia mint. Almost any piney knew how to make charcoal, and the woods were full of little clearings, which is one reason that so many culs-de-sac branch from the sand roads. Full-time colliers specialized in charcoal to the exclusion of most of the other occupations in the yearly cycle. They frequently made their pits with someone else's wood. They moved around a lot, nomadically, living in shacks that had no floors, or in tepee-shaped structures made of cedar poles and turf. They stored their supplies—mainly salt pork and apple whiskey —in turf-covered dugouts, in which they hid and sometimes died when wildfires overcame the forest. Charcoal pits were actually aboveground. They had the shape of beehives and were twenty feet high. To make them, colliers stacked cordwood in vertical tiers and covered the wood with chunks of sandy turf, known as floats. The colliers dropped burning kindling into a hole in the top and then sealed it over. They poked holes in the sides with a stick called a fagan, and kept watch over the pit day and night. If blue smoke came out, too much oxygen was involved in the combustion, and the colliers plugged a few holes. If white steam came out, the wood inside was charring perfectly. This went on for about ten days.

The late George Crummel, the Indian collier of Jenkins Neck, had a dog that could watch a pit and would awaken him if the ventilating holes needed attention. With Crummel gone, there are only two or three colliers left in the Pine Barrens. The last important market was for bagged charcoal for back-yard cooking, but the modern briquette has all but eliminated that. Most "charcoal" briquettes are made in gasoline refineries as a petroleum by-product. On this subject, Fred Brown said one day, "These here charcoal brick-a-bats, or whatever you call them, that they sell—look at them, all you have to do is *look* at them. You *know* they didn't come from no tree."

Venison, of course, was available the year round to pineys, who have always felt detached about game laws. The sphagnum-blueberry-cranberry-wood-and-charcoal cycle was supplemented in other ways as well—most notably in December, when shiploads of holly, laurel, mistletoe, ground pine, greenbriar, inkberry, plume grass, and boughs of pitch pine were sent to New York for sale as Christmas decorations. Small birch trees were cut in short lengths and turned into candleholders. People who specialized in pine cones became known as pineballers, and the term is still used. The Christmas business continues to be an important source of income in the pines. Modern pineballers pick about three thousand cones in a day. They like to get them from the dwarf forests—the Plains, as they are called—because the trees there are shorter than men, and can be picked clean. At the moment, pineballing is not as remunerative as huckleberrying. Pineballers are getting only three dollars and seventy-five cents per thousand cones, or about eleven dollars for a day's work. Pineys once sold rosin, turpentine, pitch tar, and shoemaker's wax. They cut laurel stems to sell to makers of pipes. They dug the roots of wild indigo for medicinal use (wild indigo is, among other things, a stimulant), and they cut the bark of wild cherry (a tonic) and collected pipsissewa leaves (an astringent). They sold laurel, ilex, and rhododendron to landscape gardeners. They sent wild flowers into the cities—trailing arbutus, swamp pinks, wild magnolias, lupine, azaleas, Pine Barrens gentians. They made birdhouses out of cedar slabs, and they still do. They sold box turtles by the gross to people in Philadelphia, who used the turtles to keep cellars free of snails—a market that has declined.

While isolation in the woods was bringing out self-reliance, it was also contributing to other developments that eventually attracted more attention. After the pine towns lost touch, to a large extent, with the outside world, some of the people slid into illiteracy, and a number slid further than that. Marriages were pretty casual in the pines late in the nineteenth century and early in the twentieth. For lawful weddings, people had to travel beyond the woods, to a place like Mt. Holly. Many went to native "squires," who performed weddings for a fee of one dollar. No questions were asked, even if the squires recognized the brides and the grooms as people they had married to other people a week or a month before. Given the small population of the pines, the extreme rarity of new people coming in, and the long span of time that most families had been there, some relationships were extraordinarily complicated and a few were simply incestuous. To varying degrees, there was a relatively high incidence in the pines of what in the terms of the era was called degeneracy, feeblemindedness, or mental deficiency.

In 1913, startling publicity was given to the most unfortunate stratum of the pine society, and the effects have not yet faded. In that year, Elizabeth Kite, a psychological researcher, published a report called "The Pineys," which had resulted from two years of visits to cabins in the pines. Miss Kite worked for the Vineland Training School, on the southern edge of the Pine Barrens, where important early work was being done with people of subnormal intelligence, and she was a fearless young woman who wore spotless white dresses as she rode in a horse-drawn wagon through the woods. Her concern for the people there became obvious to the people themselves, who grew fond of her, and even dependent upon her, and a colony for the care of the "feebleminded" was founded in the northern part of the Pine Barrens as a result of her work. Her report told of children who shared their bedrooms with pigs, of men who could not count beyond three, of a mother who walked nine miles with her children almost every day to get whiskey, of a couple who took a wheelbarrow with them when they went out drinking, so that one could wheel the other home. "In the heart of the region, scattered in widely

separated huts over miles of territory, exists today a group of human beings as distinct in morals and manners as to excite curiosity and wonder in the mind of any outsider brought into contact with them," Miss Kite wrote. "They are recognized as a distinct people by the normal communities living on the borders of their forests." The report included some extremely gnarled family trees, such as one headed by Sam Bender, who conceived a child with his daughter, Mollie Bender Brooks, whose husband, Billie Brooks, sometimes said the child had been fathered by his wife's brother rather than her father, both possibilities being strong ones. When a district nurse was sent around to help clean up Mollie's house, chickens and a pig were found in the kitchen, and the first implement used in cleaning the house was a hoe. Mollie, according to Miss Kite, was "good-looking and sprightly, which fact, coupled with an utter lack of sense of decency, made her attractive even to men of otherwise normal intelligence." When Billie and all of their children were killed in a fire, Mollie said cheerfully, "Well, they was all insured. I'm still young and can easy start another family." Miss Kite reported some relationships that are almost impossible to follow. Of the occupants of another cabin, she wrote, "That May should call John 'Uncle' could be accounted for on the basis of a childish acceptance of 'no-matter-what' conditions, for the connection was that her mother was married to the brother of John's other woman's second man, and her mother's sister had had children by John. This bond of kinship did not, however, keep the families long together." Miss Kite also told of a woman who came to ask for food at a state almshouse on a bitter winter day. The people at the almshouse gave her a large burlap sack containing a basket of potatoes, a basket of turnips, three cabbages, four pounds of pork, five pounds of rye flour, two pounds of sugar, and some tea. The woman shouldered the sack and walked home cross-country through snow. Thirty minutes after she reached her home, she had a baby. No one helped her deliver it, nor had anyone helped her with the delivery of her nine other children.

Miss Kite's report was made public. Newspapers printed excerpts from it. All over the state, people became alarmed about conditions in the Pine Barrens—a region most of them had never heard of. James T. Fielder, the governor of New Jersey, travelled to the pines, returned to Trenton, and sought to increase his political momentum by recommending to the legislature that the Pine Barrens be somehow segregated from the rest of New Jersey in the interest of the health and safety of the people of the state at large. "I have been shocked at the conditions I have found," he said. "Evidently these people are a serious menace to the State of New Jersey because they produce so many persons that inevitably become public charges. They have inbred, and led lawless and scandalous lives, till they have become a race of imbeciles, criminals, and defectives." Meanwhile, H. H. Goddard, director of the research laboratory at the Vineland Training School and Miss Kite's immediate superior, had taken the genealogical charts that Miss Kite had painstakingly assembled, pondered them, extrapolated a bit, and published what became a celebrated treatise on a family called Kallikak—a name that Goddard said he had invented to avoid doing harm to real people. According to the theory set forth in the treatise, nearly all pineys were descended from one man. This man, Martin Kallikak, conceived an illegitimate son with an imbecile barmaid. Martin's bastard was said to be the forebear of generations of imbeciles, prostitutes, epileptics, and drunks. Martin himself, however, married a normal girl, and among their progeny were generations of normal and intelligent people, including doctors, lawyers, politicians, and a president of Princeton University. Goddard coined the name Kallikak from the Greek *kalós* and *kakós*— "good" and "bad." Goddard's work has been discredited, but its impact, like that of Governor Fielder's proposal to segregate the Pine Barrens, was powerful in its time. Even Miss Kite seemed to believe that there was some common flaw in the blood of all the people of the pines. Of one pinelands woman, Miss Kite wrote, "Strangely enough, this woman belonged originally to good stock. No piney blood flowed in her veins."

The result of all this was a stigma that has never worn off. A surprising number of people in New Jersey today seem to think that the Pine Barrens are dark backlands inhabited by hostile and semi-literate people who would as soon shoot an outsider as look at him. A policeman in Trenton who had never been to the pines—"only driven through on the way downa shore," as people usually say —once told me, in an anxious tone, that if I intended to spend a lot of time in the Pine Barrens I was asking for trouble. Some of the gentlest of people—botanists, canoe-men, campers—spend a great deal of time in the pines, but their influence has not been sufficient to correct an impression, vivid in some parts of the state for fifty years, that the pineys are weird and sometimes dangerous bare-foot people who live in caves, marry their sisters, and eat snakes. Pineys are, for the most part, mild and shy, but their resentment is deep, and they will readily and force-fully express it. The unfortunate people that Miss Kite described in her report were a minor fraction of the total population of the Pine Barrens, and the larger number suffered from it, and are still suffering from it. This ap-palled Elizabeth Kite, who said to an interviewer in 1940, some years before her death, "Nothing would give me greater pleasure than to correct the idea that has unfor-tunately been given by the newspapers regarding the pines. Anybody who lived in the pines was a piney. I think it a most terrible calamity that the newspapers publicly took the term and gave it the degenerate sting. Those families who were not potential state cases did not interest me as far as my study was concerned. I have no language in which I can express my admiration for the pines and the people who live there."

The people of the Pine Barrens turn cold when they hear the word "piney" spoken by anyone who is not a native. Over the years since 1913, in many places outside the pines, the stigma of degeneracy has been concentrated in that word. A part of what hurts them is that they them-selves are fond of the word. They refer to one another freely, and frequently, as pineys. They have a strong regional pride, and, in a way that is not at all unflattering to them, they *are* different from the run of the people of the state. A visitor who stays awhile in the Pine Barrens soon feels that he is in another country, where attitudes and ambitions are at variance with the American norm. People who drive around in the pines and see houses like Fred Brown's, with tarpaper peeling from the walls, and automobiles overturned in the front yard, often decide, as they drive on, that they have just looked destitution in the face. I wouldn't call it that. I have yet to meet any-one living in the Pine Barrens who has in any way indicated envy of people who live elsewhere. One reason there are so many unpainted houses in the Pine Barrens is that the pineys believe, correctly, that their real-estate assessments would be higher if their houses were painted. Some pineys who make good money in blueberries or cranberries or in jobs on the outside would never think of painting their houses. People from other parts of New Jersey will say of Pine Barrens people, "They don't like to work. They can't seem to hold jobs." This, too, is a judgment based on outside values. What the piney usually says is "I hate to be tied down long to any one job." That remark is made so often in the pines that it is almost a local slogan. It expresses an attitude born of the old pines cycle—sphagnum in the spring, berries in the summer, coaling when the weather is cold. With the plenitude of the woodland around them—and, historically, behind them —pineys are bored with the idea of doing the same thing all year long, in every weather. Many of them have to, of course. Many work at regular jobs outside the woods. But many try that and give it up, preferring part-time labor—always at rest in the knowledge that no one who knows the woods and is willing to do a little work on his own is ever going to go hungry. The people have no difficulty articulating what it is that gives them a special feeling about the landscape they live in; they know that their environment is unusual and they know why they value it. Some, of course, put it with more finesse than others do. "I'm just a woods boy," a fellow named Jim Leek said to me one day. "There ain't nobody bothers you here. You can be alone. I'm just a woods boy. I wouldn't want to live in a town." When he said "town," he meant one of the small communities in the pines; he preferred living in the woods to living in a Pine Barrens town. When pineys talk about going to "the city," they usually mean Mt. Holly or the Moorestown Mall or the Two Guys from Harrison store on Route 206. When Jim Leek said "nobody bothers you" and "you can be alone," he was sounding two primary themes of the pines. Bill Wasovwich said one day, "The woods just look nice and it's more quieter. It's quiet anywhere in the pines. That's why I like it here." Another man, Scorchy Jones, who works for the state Fish and Game Division, said this to an interviewer from a small New Jersey radio station: "A sense of security is high among us. We were from pioneers. We know how to survive in the woods. Here in these woods areas, you have a reputation. A dishonest person can't survive in the community. You have to maintain your reputation, or you would have to jump from place to place. A man lives by his reputation and by his honesty and by his ambition to work. If he doesn't have it, he would be an outcast. These people have the reputations of their parents and grandparents ahead of them—and they are proud of them, and they want to maintain that same standard. They don't worship gold. All they want is necessities. They would rather live than make a lot of money. They live by this code. They're the best citizens in this country." Later in the interview, Jones said, "Unless these wild areas are preserved, we're going to get to the point where dense population is going to work on the nervous systems of the people, and the more that takes place, the poorer neighbors they become. Eventually, like birds or animals confined to too small an area, they will fight among themselves. Man is an animal as well." People known in the pines as "the old-time pineys"—those who lived wholly by the cycle, and seldom, if ever, saw an outsider—are gone now. When the United States Army built Camp Dix on the northwestern edge of the Pine Barrens during the First World War, civilian jobs were created, and many people of the pines first got to know what money was and how to use it. Paved roads first crossed the pines in the nineteen-twenties. Electrical lines, the Second World War, and television successively brought an end to the utter isolation of the pineys. But so far all this has not materially changed their attitudes. They are apparently a tolerant people, with an attractive spirit of live and let live. They seem to like hard work, if not steady work, and they like to brag about working hard. When they say they will do something, they do it. They seem shy, like the people who went before them, but when they get to know an outsider they are not shy and will generously share their tables, which often include new-potato stews and cranberry potpies. I have met Pine Barrens people who have, at one time or another, moved to other parts of the country. Most of them tried other lives for a while, only to return unreluctantly to the pines. One of them explained to me, "It's a privilege to live in these woods."

4

The Air Tune

THE VERNACULAR LANGUAGE OF THE
pines is splendidly metaphorical. An outsider needs a
glossary to follow simple directions—for example, "Go
down here about a mile and turn left at the fingerboard."
A fingerboard is a place where several roads come together. A point is a place where a road forks. When highway workers do anything to a road, they are said to be
sciencing it. One day while I was driving along with
Fred Brown, he said, "I didn't know this road was oiled
all the way to here." The road was covered with pave-
ment. Applejack is the laureate liquid of the pines. It is
known as jack, and its effects are known as apple palsy.
Pineys are much more imaginative than non-pineys with
the common names of plants and flowers. There is a plant
in the Pine Barrens that has velvety, magical leaves to
which water absolutely will not adhere. Its common
name is golden club. The pineys call it neverwet. Another
plant, an *Arenaria*, is small and beautiful, and on its white
flowers there is always a shining fluid. The plant's common name is sandwort. The pineys call it sparkle. They

even have a better name than lady's-slipper. This small and exquisite orchid grows in the pines, where the natives call it a whippoorwill shoe. Of course, every last piney, shown a lady's-slipper, would not say, "That is a whippoorwill shoe." The Pine Barrens are too vast for that, and much of the pines vernacular is sub-regional. I doubt if Fred Brown would know a whippoorwill shoe from a lily of the valley; and, for all I know, he may be the only man in the pines who calls whiskey rum. At least, he is the only one I have ever heard call whiskey rum, but I have heard him say it many times. When he drinks his rum straight, or neat, he says he is drinking it clear. Fred refers to guardrails—the things that run along beside highways to protect cars—as guardrails. Many pineys call them bannisters. Soft sand is called sugar sand, and when a car gets stuck in it, the car is said to be set. The people say "thataway" and "tater" and "I ain't a-gonna." They also say "passed away." Homes are sometimes called homesteads. A native guide is a woodjin. Grouse are called pheasants. The pine trees themselves—the predominant pitch pines, at any rate—are called Old Jersey Bull Pines. Whenever Fred Brown referred to a man's wife—including, on one occasion, the wife of the President of the United States—he said "his woman." Fred says "spragnum" for "sphagnum," "braken" for "bracken," and "fastly" for "quickly," and when he was telling me that he had never flown in a plane he said, "I could of flewn lots of times, but I never cared to." In Tuckerton one day, he stopped a man to ask directions of him, and he said, "Excuse me, are you acquainted here?" In the vernacular, a low, wet area where the Atlantic white cedars grow is called a cripple. If no cedars grow there, the wet area is called a spong, which is pronounced to rhyme with "sung." Some people define spongs and cripples a little differently, saying that water always flows in a cripple but there is water in a spong only after a rain. Others say that any lowland area where highbush blueberries grow is a spong. With all this, it is no wonder that the names of places in the pines are so distinctive. In the nineteenth century, a man named Jacob Ong— whose name was pronounced conventionally, like "song" or "long"—went to a dance in a village in the northern part of the pines, and he somehow infuriated one of his partners, and she pulled Ong's hat from his head and crunched it under her feet. Ong is said to have taken the hat and tossed it up into a tree, where it caught on a branch and remained for months. The settlement below became known as Ong's Hat. It is one of the vanished towns, but cartographers find it irresistible, and it still appears on road maps. Once, in the eastern pines, there was a cranberry dam that kept giving way, and whenever it did one of the cranberry workers said, "Here's trouble." Then the dam gave way twice in a single week, and when this happened the man said, "Here's double trouble." That particular bog, which was run for years by the Double Trouble Cranberry Company, has been bought by the State of New Jersey, along with two thousand acres of surrounding land. It is now Double Trouble State Park.

Fred Brown told me one day that in modern times

there have been certain adjustments in the ways that some of the older Pine Barrens families pronounce their names. "The Browers used to pronounce their name Brewer," he said. "They're still Brewers as far as I'm concerned, but they say they're Browers. It ain't changed them any, so far as I can see. The Jervises call themselves Jarvises now. The Salmons used to pronounce it Simons. Fifteen to twenty years ago, they started calling themselves Salmons." There is not much that Fred could do with the name Brown, even if he were inclined to, but his great-grandfather Zachariah Jenkins was the man for whom Jenkins and Jenkins Neck were named, and Fred is quick to point this out. Fred was born in Jenkins on June 29, 1887. His father did several things but was chiefly a cabinet-finisher. The school where Fred helped to plant the red cedar tree was near the Godfrey Bridge on the Wading River. "I made the fifth reader," Fred said. "That's the highest one there was in the school at that time. From what I've heard, it would be equal to the eighth grade today." He finished school at the age of fifteen. He worked with his father, as a carpenter, for a while. He also became skilled as a sawyer and worked in sawmills. "I cut cedar, I growed cranberries, I worked for construction companies, I gathered wild huckleberries, wild cranberries, moss—I pulled, I expect, two or three hundred carloads of moss," he said. "The only laws I ever used—if I was hungry and wanted a pheasant or a deer or something, I went out and killed it." When Fred was young, the now vanished towns were still vanishing, and he remembers the last people who lived in them. In

Washington, for example, he said to me one day, "Jim Snow's was the last house. I went to school with Jim Snow's son and his daughter. It was a good house. Jim Snow's daughter runs Jennings' bar, in Indian Mills. She is two years older than I am. Right there is where she was born, and don't let her tell you she wasn't." In Martha once, standing under the old catalpa trees, with their long-podded seeds hanging down above us, Fred said, "The big mansion was there. I eat chicken potpie in that mansion. Aunt Katie Gunner was the last person to live here, in the mansion here under these bean trees." In 1910, Fred married a girl named Elizabeth Mick. They raised their seven children first in Jenkins and then in the house where Fred now lives in Hog Wallow. Elizabeth Brown died in 1948 and is buried in the pines, where Fred will be buried. Their children are now, in descending order of age, a housewife in a town on the edge of the pines, a retired state policeman, a guard in a juvenile home near the pines, a mechanic, a laborer for the state highway department, a wild-huckleberry picker and part-time junkman, and a beautician in Alexandria, Virginia. Fred himself was for many years—from 1915 to 1952—a cranberry broker. Dressed in overalls, he went around in horse-drawn wagons, then in Model Ts. He bought cranberries in the bogs and took them to canneries on the periphery of the Pine Barrens. "One was to New Egypt," he told me. "One was to Williamstown. One was to Folsom. One was to Egg Harbor. And one was to Landisville." These canneries eventually became part of the interstate coöperative Ocean Spray. Fred was also a blueberry broker, and he had his own small bogs and fields. "I just happen to be the one man in the State of New Jersey that growed seventeen straight crops of cranberries," he said once when we were riding along on a cranberry dam in my car. He explained that cranberry growers usually have to let their bogs be idle in one of every seven years. They do this by leaving the bogs flooded through blossom time, which is around the Fourth of July. Most bogs lose their vitality after about six years of growing and need a year of renewal.

"I believe they get that seven years out of the Bible," Bill Wasovwich said, from the back seat. "That seven years is in the Bible."

"I used fertilize and light sand," Fred said. "That will do it."

A fairly uncomplicated machine now knocks cranberries off the vines at harvest time, but the day of the hand cranberry scoop is so recent that Bill, at twenty-eight, is remembered as the last of the champion scoopers. He picks at his nails modestly when this is said, but it is apparently true. Growers told me Bill worked so hard that they had to go out into the bogs at dusk and actually take the scoop from his hands in order to force him to stop for the day. Fred says that he, too, was a great picker in his time. "I seen a Portugee scoop a half-barrel box in less than two minutes," he told me. "The best I could do was three minutes. There wasn't another man out of eighty that could scoop one in three minutes." Field, bog, and forest, Fred once owned five hundred and seventy-five acres, in Jenkins and in Hog Wallow. Now he owns one acre.

At Fred's house one day, Bill asked me if I would like to go down the road and see his bog. On the way, we stopped at his cabin. It is a small, sturdy saltbox in the woods, perhaps eighteen feet on a side. Bill had then lived in it for three years. It was clean within, and almost empty. An enamelled cabinet, a kerosene stove, and a small table were the only pieces of furniture in the room. Leaning against the doorjamb was a high-velocity rifle. A kerosene lamp on the table had been in the same position for a long time, for up the wall behind it went a wide and thick V of lampblack that pooled into a black hemisphere on the ceiling. Beside the lamp on the table was a huge book, larger than a Webster's New International Dictionary. It was open, and strewn all over it and the rest of the table were sheets of lined white paper covered with writing.

The first thing I asked Bill after we went into the cabin was where he slept, because there was no bed or cot.

"On the floor," he said. "I have a sleeping bag."

I then asked what the book was.

Bill said that it was a Bible and that he was taking a Bible correspondence course from Ambassador College. He was in the middle of the eighth course he had taken in Biblical studies. The enormous Bible was the largest he had been able to buy. He said it had cost twenty-seven dollars, and he explained that he needed large type so that he could read in the kerosene light at night. I picked up the heavy rifle and balanced it in my hands. Bill said it was a 44/40 Winchester, a model first built in 1873, and that it fired big, two-hundred-grain bullets. Unfortunately, he went on, the cartridges cost eight and a half dollars for a box of fifty, so he couldn't use the rifle very often. When he treats himself to a box of bullets, he does not space out the pleasure. He prefers to shoot up the whole boxful as rapidly as he can. The rifle has lever action and holds fifteen shells at a time. Bill selects a target, frequently nothing more than a pine tree, and rips it with fifty bullets. Sometimes the bullets cut the tree down. For other purposes, he said, he had only used the rifle three times—once to kill a dog, once to kill a deer, and once to frighten a reporter, who drove up in a car that had the name of a Trenton newspaper on it, got out, and peered through a window into Bill's cabin, in an attempt—Bill thought—to see how pineys live. Bill picked up the rifle, and the reporter ran to his car and drove away. "I'd have never shot to kill him," Bill told me. "But I'd have threw lead at him if I'd been scared enough. I wasn't scared enough."

Bill's bog is small—four acres. He only has time for it when he is not at work in other men's bogs, and for more than two years he has been clearing it and building up its dams by hand. The forest edges it on three sides, another bog on the fourth. Among the trees that line Bill's land are white birches and dark cedars. It is a pretty corner in the pines. Bill's hope is that he will marry, build a home there, and raise a family. "I intend to build a house down my bog or die trying it, I can tell you that," he said.

I asked him if the land was actually his.

He said that his employer had given it to him, but that he had no deed. "It's as good as my bog," he went on. "They can't take it away from me. They could, legally. But they'd have to get the state troopers. They take this bog, they take me with it. I'll get up here with my rifle. I took out stumps in here the size of chairs."

Bill spent one year in high school, in a town just outside the pines. For a number of years after that, while he was working in cranberry bogs and blueberry fields, he drove cars and pickup trucks without a driver's license. One day, when Bill was driving too fast in a pickup he had, he saw a state trooper approaching him from behind, and he put his foot to the floor and started a chase, which the trooper lost because Bill led him through a series of bogs and eventually set him in sugar sand. Unfortunately for Bill, the trooper had read his plates. Bill was soon arrested and put in jail for seventy days. Disgusted with life, Bill sold his pickup for a hundred dollars and caught a Greyhound bus for the pinelands of Georgia, where he cut pulpwood near Waycross and Fargo for about a year. He became so lonely that he took another Greyhound north to New Jersey. "When I came back, I was never so glad to see anything as these woods," he told me.

I asked him if he was going to be married soon.

"Who to?" he said. "I been looking for ten years. Like my father, I'm no good. I've always been ascared of girls, all my life." He went on to say that at one time there had been a girl he was fond of, but he had never taken her out. "The bravest I got was to talk to her once," he said. Bill carves Indian dolls out of wood, and he would like to give them to a girl, but he knows no one he can give them to.

One day, Fred Brown told Bill and me that when he was eighteen he liked his women in the age range of fifteen to sixty-two. He also told us a story about a fight he once had over a woman. He said he had been "jumped by three guys" one night when he walked into the Peacock Inn, in Chatsworth, a pine town about six miles north of Hog Wallow. "The girl—they wanted her, she wouldn't have them," he said. "They couldn't go with her. I could. They had all tried me singlehanded and they knowed they couldn't handle me one at a time. Ander Bozarth got his jaw broke. I throwed him across the pool table and his head hit the pocket that was iron. Bill Green—I throwed him over the bar and he went right into the big barrel full of bottled beer and ice. Bill Ford was next. Howard Sooy, who was watching—he was a friend of mine—he couldn't stand to see three on one. He grabbed Bill Ford and knocked him out. I was eighteen. I would say the girl was around forty." Fred brags winningly. One reason he is so good at it is that bragging is an honored craft where he lives, an element in the general art of storytelling, which was once of enough importance in the Pine Barrens to give rise to a class of local Homers, some of whom did nothing at all but travel through the woods telling tales. Big Bill Estell, who died in 1882, told stories for a living, and explained to people that he was too heavy for light work and too light for heavy work. Cracky Wainwright—whose name, in the pines, is pronounced Wineright—went around telling stories and stopped off at his own house once a year. Ander Bozarth, the fellow whose jaw Fred Brown disassembled in Chatsworth, was a male Scheherazade, known for his ability to tell a different story every night for months. Stories were told beside burning charcoal, and beside bonfires that used to blaze at night in cranberry-harvest time, when, before the automobile, pineys slept in the woods near the bogs they were working in. Most stories at least began with truth, but some never gave it a nod.

In the late nineteen-thirties and early nineteen-forties, a graduate student from the English Department of Indiana University went around the Pine Barrens collecting stories. He was motivated in part by the somewhat melancholy knowledge that the development of broadcasting was going to wash away much of this part of regional American life. The student, Herbert N. Halpert, is now a professor of English at Memorial University, in Newfoundland. His doctoral dissertation was called "Folktales and Legends from the New Jersey Pines." He dated each story he heard. On June 19, 1941, a piney named Charles Grant told Halpert, "I heard old Cracky Wainright say he seen two black snakes come together, and they was both mad. He seen they was going to fight, so he stood and watched them. The one got ahold of the other one's tail and began to swallow it. And the other one got ahold of the other one's tail and began to swallow *him*. He said they kept on fighting and swallowing one another until both snakes was swallowed. There wasn't *any* snake left there at all." Grant also told Halpert a story about a piney who went around for a long time claiming that he had a pair of horns in his shack seventeen feet from tip to tip. People liked this brief story and kept asking the man to tell it. Eventually, as Grant remembered it, "He said no, that was one lie he had told so much he believed it himself. He said he had told about putting the horns up in the middle of his shack so much he believed they was there. So he said the last time he was there he made up his mind he would crawl up there and see if there was anything there. He said he went up there and there they was—seventeen foot from tip to tip." On June 26, 1941, a piney named George White told Halpert, "I heard of this old fellow travelling, and he had a jug of liquor with him. Come by this pond and he was taking a drink. And the frogs hollered, 'Jug-and-all, jug-and-all.' And he threw the jug and all in, because he thought the frogs wanted jug and all." On September 1, 1942, Stacy Bozarth, a collier, told Halpert about a man who had killed a deer. "He hit him with one shot and hit him in the hind foot and hit him in the ear," Bozarth said. "Now how could he do it? Can you tell me? Well, I can tell you. Well, the deer had his hind foot up scratching his ear."

After reading these stories, I repeated them to Fred Brown, who blew air through his teeth and said he had heard them all. He said *he* could tell me a *true* story. He asked if I had heard about a couple named Will and El Nichols. "Will and El Nichols dreamed three times—this ain't second-handed, this is first-handed—they dreamed three nights straight that there was an iron-handled drawer buried up to Tulpehocken, on the road that goes from the Joe Holloway Field and comes out to the High Crossing. They dreamed that there was a box there—with an iron drawer in it—near an old-fashioned walnut tree right along the road. Neither one told the other that they had dreamed anything. One morning, they got up and Will said to El, 'I'm going up to Tulpehocken.' 'So am I,' said El. They went up, and dug, and found a box full of buckskin bags full of gold coins. I've seen the hole where they dug that out. They would never tell how much gold they got, but they had nothing before and they had money the rest of their lives, and they had it when they died. They lived down here to Bulltown." Fred had an afterthought. "People used to put gold coins in buckskin bags and bury them all over these woods," he said.

The Pine Barrens have had two Paul Bunyans and one Merlin. Jesse Johnson is a local legendary figure who is said to have been seven feet tall and to have been capable of carrying two horseloads of stone. The other strongman hero was a woodchopper, and he is said to have been capable of cutting ten cords of wood in a day. His name was Salt Caesar. The wizard of the pines was Jerry Munyhon. He could make a cat's paw come through a keyhole. He could cause axes to chop wood by themselves. He could cause money to multiply. He was bulletproof. And he once caught a bullet that was fired at him and handed it to the man who had done the shooting. From some distance away, Munyhon could cause a man to stop in his tracks. Munyhon's cane was superior to Toulouse-

Lautrec's. Munyhon's cane, on its own, could *go and get* whiskey. Munyhon is said to have lived in one of the iron towns, and to have died in the eighteen-sixties. Once, he asked for work at an iron furnace and was turned down. He stopped the furnace by causing it to fill with black and white crows. He got the job, and the crows flew away. Munyhon once came upon a six-mule team that was trying, unsuccessfully, to pull a wagon with a huge boiler on it up a hill. He had a Leghorn rooster under his arm, and he tied it to the tongue of the wagon and said, "Shoo!" The rooster pulled the load up and over the hill. Of all his powers, Munyhon's most widely celebrated one was a remarkable ability to create in the minds of women the illusion that they were walking in thigh-deep water when in fact they were walking on dry land. Up went their skirts.

Munyhon's water trick has parallels that go back as far as King Solomon, who pulled a similar trick on the Queen of Sheba. His horsepowered rooster has antecedents in the lore of several European nations. European sources can be found for many of the legends of the pines. In America, the Pine Barrens have been a kind of cultural middle ground, where regional traditions overlap. Halpert wrote in his dissertation, for example, "This region is the meeting place for the Northern and Southern folk-song traditions. Certain songs and ballads are found in New England and other Northern states. Others are encountered only in the Southern states. In South Jersey, the various tides of immigration met, and here one often finds a husband and wife, one singing the Northern

variances and the other the Southern, each of course in-
sisting that his or her version is the true one." Men who
sing have always been particularly respected in the Pine
Barrens, where the test of a singer's repertory is: Can
he sing from morning until evening without repeating
himself? Pineys once made violins out of red maple from
the swamps. Sam Giberson (1808-84), known throughout the pines as Fiddler Sammy Buck, one night told a
group of people that he thought he could beat any com-
petitor both as a fiddler and as a dancer—"and," he went
on, "I think I can beat the Devil." On his way home,
Giberson met the Devil himself at a bridge. The Devil
told him to play his violin, and while Giberson played
the Devil danced. Then the Devil played the violin while
Giberson danced. Giberson was the kind of dancer of
whom people said things like "I seen him put a looking
glass on the floor and dance on it—he was that light when
he danced." But the Devil danced even more lightly and
beautifully than Giberson, and the Devil played the
violin more sweetly. Giberson conceded defeat. The
Devil then said that he was going to take Giberson to
Hell unless he could play a tune that the Devil had never
heard. Out of the air, by Giberson's account, a tune came
to him—a beautiful theme that neither Giberson nor the
Devil had ever heard. The Devil let him go. That is what
Giberson told people on the following day and for the
rest of his life. The tune is known in the Pine Barrens
as Sammy Giberson's Air Tune. No one, of course,
knows how it goes, but the Air Tune is there, every-

where, just beyond hearing. Giberson drank a lot, like many of the fiddlers of his time.

Fred Brown said he might have competed with a man like Giberson once, but not at the age of seventy-nine. "I can't jig no more like I used to," he told me. "My legs won't twist around like they would. Wherever there was music, I used to jig. For years, we had a dance every Friday night to Chatsworth, in the hall. Now they go to a bar somewhere, and get half drunk, and go home. The younger people, they don't never waltz or two-step or time-and-a-half."

The Pine Barrens once had their own particular witch. Pineys put salt over their doors to discourage visits from the Witch of the Pines, Peggy Clevenger. It was known that she could turn herself into a rabbit, for a dog was once seen chasing a rabbit and the rabbit jumped through the window of a house, and there—in the same instant, in the window—stood Peggy Clevenger. On another occasion, a man saw a lizard and tried to kill it by crushing it with a large rock. When the rock hit the lizard, the lizard disappeared and Peggy Clevenger materialized on the spot and smacked the man in the face. Clevenger is a Hessian name. Peggy lived in Pasadena, another of the now vanished towns, about five miles east of Mt. Misery. It was said that she had a stocking full of gold. Her remains were found one morning in the smoking ruins of her cabin, but there was no trace of the gold.

The Pine Barrens also have their own monster. This creature has been feared in the woods—on a somewhat diminishing scale—from the seventeen-thirties to the present. It is known as Leeds' Devil, or the Jersey Devil, and a year or so ago the Trenton *Times* ran an article, with a Pine Barrens dateline, that said, "State Police from the Tuckerton Barracks today are searching for a wild beast. . . . Trooper Alfred Potter reported finding a footprint that was so large a man's hand could not cover it. . . . Many remember the legend of the Jersey Devil." From "a farm in a woodland swamp," the beast had carried away two large dogs, three geese, four cats, and thirty-one ducks. Remains of these animals were found, but that was all that was ever found. If the perpetrator was Leeds' Devil, the haul was modest, for Leeds' Devil had in the past been said to have devoured small children and to have mutilated strong young men. Over the years, the physical appearance and the personal history of the monster have been variously described. There are two main versions of its birth, which occurred early in the eighteenth century—one that a woman named Leeds so scornfully treated a preacher who was trying to convert her that the preacher told Mrs. Leeds her next child would be the offspring of Satan, and the other that Mrs. Leeds had so large a family that she cursed all unborn children and said she hoped she would give birth to the Devil, which she did. The Devil child's appearance was said to combine the features of a bat and a kangaroo. It was described in Cornelius Weygandt's book *Down Jersey* as "a leather-winged, steel-springed jumper of goat size that could clear a cranberry bog at a bound." (A variant was that it had a horse's head, the wings of a bat, and a serpent's tail.) It tore at its mother's flesh while it nursed.

At the age of four, it killed its mother and its father and began its terrible wanderings, cutting the throats of hogs, horses, cattle, sheep, children, women, and men, and leaving cloven tracks. People used to hang up lanterns to scare the Jersey Devil away. Most people in the Pine Barrens now look upon the Jersey Devil as pure legend, but there are many who do not. Unexplained and sinister events will still cause its name to be spoken in serious voices.

Bill Wasovwich, for his part, is not certain whether he believes or disbelieves. "I was out in a swamp once on a moonlight night," he told me. "A mist came up, laying out in there like a blanket. You've seen those nights. Fog was rising up like a thing coming through water. Something screamed. My hat flew off my head. I ran home, through briars. My arms was all cut up when I got home."

Fred Brown believes. "The Jersey Devil is real," he told me. "That is no fake story. A woman named Leeds had twelve living children. She said if she ever had another one she hoped it would be the Devil. She had her thirteenth child, and it growed, and one day it flew away. It's haunted the earth ever since. It's took pigs right out of pens. And little lambs. I believe it took a baby once, right down in Mathis town. The Leeds Devil is a crooked-faced thing, with wings. Believe what you want, I'm telling you the truth."

5

The Capital of the Pines

CHATSWORTH, IN WOODLAND TOWNSHIP, is the principal community in the Pine Barrens. It is six miles north of the approximate center of the pines at Hog Wallow, and is surrounded on all sides by deep forest. From the air, two miles away, Chatsworth is not visible under the high cover of oaks and pines. The town consists of three hundred and six people, seventy-four houses, ten trailers, a firehouse, a church, a liquor store, a post office, a school, two sawmills, and one general store. Somehow, Chatsworth is a half-tone more attractive than any other town in the pines. The people are apparently just a little competitive about the appearance of their houses, most of which are painted, and this gives Chatsworth a measure of distinction from its "suburbs" —the word used in Chatsworth for small settlements nearby in the woods, such as Leektown, Butler Place, Speedwell, and Jones Mill. People in Chatsworth pay twenty-four dollars a truckload to bring in topsoil so that they can grow lawns. That sort of thing notwithstanding, individualism and personal independence are as important there as they are in the rest of the pines. Two-thirds of Chatsworth's people make their living in Woodland Township—mainly from cranberries and blueberries and from "working for the state highway" and patrolling the woods as fire wardens or foresters. Half the people classify themselves as self-employed. Most of them are descended from English, Irish, and German ancestors who settled in the Pine Barrens in the eighteenth century, and the headstones in the Chatsworth cemetery bear names such as Brower, Bozarth, Dunfee, Leek, Applegate, Ritzendollar, and Buzby.

On the southwest corner of the town's principal intersection is the Chatsworth General Store, the entrance to which was cut into a corner of the building on an angle, so that the door itself, aproned with concrete steps, is the most prominent exterior feature of the building. The door was apparently designed to attract people from both intersecting streets, although the store has no competition for a ten-mile sweep in all directions. When I first stopped in there, I noticed on its shelves the usual run of cold cuts, canned foods, soft drinks, crackers, cookies, cereals, and sardines, and also Remington twelve-gauge shotgun shells, Slipknot friction tape, Varsity gasket cement, Railroad Mills sweet snuff, and State-Wide well restorer. Wrapping string unwound from a spool on a wall shelf and ran through eyelets across the ceiling and down to a wooden counter. A glass counter top next to the wooden one had been rubbed cloudy by hundreds of thousands of coins and pop bottles, and in the case beneath it were twenty-two rectangular glass dishes, each holding a different kind of penny candy. Beside the candy case was a radiator covered with an oak plank. Chatsworth loafers sat there. There were no particular loafers. Almost everyone who came into the store spent a little time on the oak plank. There were three Esso pumps on the sidewalk outside. Esso had been sold there since 1921. Just inside the door, a red kerosene pump was set in the floor. I was told that as many as four hundred gallons of kerosene had been sold through it in a week. Kerosene is widely used in the pines, both for heat and for light.

The general store was built in 1865. It was owned and run from 1894 until 1939 by Willis Jefferson Buzby, who was known as the King of the Pineys. After Buzby's death, the place was taken over by his son Willis Jonathan Buzby, who assumed his father's title, and who is still called the King of the Pineys, although he and his wife, Kate, recently sold the business to another Chatsworth couple and retired to their house across the street. "We're the original pineys," Mrs. Buzby said to me in the store one day. "People come here and say, 'We're looking for the pineys,' and I say, 'They're right here,' and they say, 'No, we mean the people who live in caves and intermarry,' and I say, 'I don't know of any such people. We're pineys. We live right here.' " Mrs. Buzby is a small woman with gray hair and bright eyes. "We've had electric in here since 1932," she went on. "People come here now and see all the electric fixtures and say, 'My goodness, I didn't know the pineys lived like this.' Some of these homes don't look so good on the outside, but in the inside they have everything—refrigerators, radios, television."

Her husband, who has a forward bend in his walk and is a man of quick motions, said over his shoulder as he moved off to fill an order, "I'm a piney and I'm proud of it."

"Live in caves and intermarry, hah," Mrs. Buzby went on. "No one ever lived in caves that I heard of. I don't know of anyone around here except one family that's intermarried, and I've lived here all my life. Illegitimacy is low. In the city, you can do what you like. Here, you make a misstep and everyone knows it. There are some drifters, but not many. We have very few new people in town—perhaps half a dozen."

Mrs. Buzby's maiden name was Ritzendollar. When she went to high school, in Pemberton, on the periphery of the pinelands, she stayed there during the week, and when the roads were bad in winter she had to stay in Pemberton for as much as a month without going home. Her husband went to a one-room school in Chatsworth and did not go on to high school. They have one daughter, Theresa, who married a boy she met at Pemberton High School. Their son-in-law now does acoustical research at the University of Michigan. The Buzbys have two granddaughters. One went to Radcliffe and majored in art, married a graduate of the Harvard Medical School, and lives in Palo Alto, California. The other is now at Wellesley. A Wellesley banner was tacked to a canned-goods shelf in the Chatsworth General Store.

On the store bulletin board was a proclamation signed

by Peter T. Brower, mayor of Woodland Township, forbidding all men to shave for six weeks. Violators would be fined two dollars, which would be used to help cover the costs of a coming celebration of the centennial of the township's incorporation. Almost every man in Chatsworth had grown a grisly stubble. Buzby had let his own beard go for the better part of a week. Now he got out an electric razor and plugged it into an outlet. "I better shave," he said, rubbing the machine against his face. "I look like a God-damned Rip van Winkle. It costs you two bucks to shave now."

Out of a mud-colored 1948 De Soto came an old woman in a gray dress that reached her ankles. She bought two cans of beans and one slab of uncut bacon. She complained to Mrs. Buzby about a slab of bacon she had bought two weeks before, and she went out.

An old man in a straw hat, a faded blue shirt, and khaki trousers stopped in for his Philadelphia *Inquirer*. He reminisced with Mrs. Buzby. They talked of the school they went to, in Chatsworth, years ago. There was a big coal stove in the middle of the schoolroom. The oldest boys could throw erasers hard enough to knock the stovepipe out of the wall. When a doctor was scheduled to visit the school, the children ran into the woods to avoid vaccinations. The old man complained bitterly about a teacher who had whipped him for someone else's misdemeanor. As the old man was leaving, Mrs. Buzby drew him out on the origin of the word "pineys." He said, "Pineys is a freak name that was invented in New York City."

A Ford station wagon stopped at one of the Esso pumps, and Mrs. Peter Brower, the wife of the Mayor, pumped herself three dollars and seventy cents' worth of gas. She waved at Buzby and drove away. Buzby got out a book, read the pump from inside the store, and recorded what Brower owed.

An old blue-and-white Chevrolet succeeded Mrs. Brower at the pumps. In it was a tan and extremely tired-looking young woman with long tawny hair. She wore a green blouse. Two small children were crawling on her. Buzby went out. She undid two of her blouse buttons and reached inside. She removed a bill, unfolded it, and handed it to Buzby. He pumped a dollar's worth of gas.

A young man wearing a sleeveless shirt and dungarees asked Mrs. Buzby for a pack of cigarettes and a soft drink. "That will be fifty cents out of your jeans," she said.

Buzby, who frequently addressed remarks not to one person but to the loitering audience in general, announced that he had never had a drink or a smoke. "I got the thirty cents and I can do what I damned please with it," he said.

Charlie Applegate, custodian of the Chatsworth school and the husband of a teacher there, sat down on the oak plank for a while. In the course of a conversation, he told me that he once made seven hundred dollars in six weeks gathering wild blueberries. He is tanned, has gray hair, and speaks softly. He has a canoe, and loves to spend his free time on Pine Barrens rivers. "The woods are not built up, because they're so far from everything," he said. "In ten or fifteen years, they're going to build up. There's a proposal for a jetport. Most of the younger people are for it. The older people are not."

Buzby entered the conversation, saying, "As I look at it, damned if I'd want a jetport out there. It's going to be God-damned noisy."

"People from all over moving in would create problems," Applegate went on. "We have no crimes here. *That* would come to an end."

The statement—often heard in the Pine Barrens—that there is no crime in the pines is essentially true, with only a few exceptions, but among these exceptions some absorbing practices and events have been recorded. Fifty years ago, mounted state police patrolled the pines from barracks in Chatsworth. Now state police from barracks outside the woods patrol the pines, but only as a minor part of their work, which is almost wholly taken up with problems that arise elsewhere. A trooper at the Red Lion barracks, west of the woods, said to me one day, "There's no crime rate at all in the pines. They're loners in there. They don't bother you. You don't bother them. They take care of most of their troubles by themselves." Criminal events involving local people are infrequent. In 1912, a cranberry grower was returning to his bog with money to pay his scoopers when he came to a bridge that had been barricaded on the road from Atsion to Hampton Furnace. The men who had set up the barricade shot the grower and took the money. People still talk about it. Fred Brown once took me to the bridge and pantomimed the crime as he imagined it had happened. A man disappeared from Chatsworth in 1947, his bones were found in 1954, and the case has never been solved or explained. Two old men in Chatsworth fought over a woman in 1963, and one murdered the other. Stickups are all but unthinkable in the pines. Tavernkeepers and storekeepers say that the possibility almost never crosses their minds, and never did at all before the night in 1964 when a man with a silk stocking over his head and a gun in his hand walked into Hedger House, a bar isolated in the woods three miles north of Chatsworth. The man said that he wanted all the money in the cash register. By the accounts of those who were there, the men at the bar looked at the holdup man in surprise and disbelief. After a long moment in which nothing happened, except that one man is said to have continued his drinking, there was an explosion of gunfire from the back of the room and the holdup man fell to the floor and died.

Moonshining has been practiced in the pines for more years than there has been an Internal Revenue Service, but it is done only on a mild scale today. The trooper at Red Lion told me, "All they have to do is dig a hole in the ground four feet deep and set up a still in a swamp. I've only been on two still raids in my life, but that's how they set it up. We don't go looking for moonshiners, to tell you the truth." Any fruit or grain will make whiskey, and the pineys use blueberries, apples, corn, or peaches. Sometimes outsiders come in—from places like Perth Amboy, Jersey City, Newark, or New York—and

set up big-syndicate stills at dead ends of the sand roads. Such stills are highly efficient alcohol plants, which cost about fifty thousand dollars. They last a short time, usually, while Cadillacs move in and out of the pines carrying hoods who think they are alone in the remotest place they have ever seen. But all the time they are being watched by the pineys, who tell the police. Syndicate moonshiners could spoil the woods for small-scale, native moonshiners, and the moonshiners of the Pine Barrens have always made extraordinary efforts to keep their forest, for their purposes, free and clear. The age of blimps is over now, but not long ago blimps in great numbers were based at Lakehurst Naval Air Station, on the northeastern border of the central pinelands, and it was common for the big airships to return to Lakehurst with holes in their envelopes. As the blimps hung over the woods, moonshiners frequently shot at them, in the mistaken belief that the sailors in them were sweeping the woods with binoculars in search of stills.

I once asked David Harrison, the chief fire warden of the Pine Barrens area, how many moonshiners are in the pines today.

"We don't know," he said. "We leave them alone. They leave us alone. Look at it this way: If we go in there and report them and they get arrested, they might spend six months in jail; then when they come out—if they wanted to get even—they could burn down half of New Jersey."

When crime occurs in the Pine Barrens, it is usually the work of outsiders, for whom the woods hold sinister attractions simply because they are so vast. From a gangland point of view, it makes better sense to put a body in the Pine Barrens than in the Hudson River. Another state trooper said to me, "Anybody who wanted to commit a murder—all he'd have to do is ride back there with a shovel. They'd never find that body. I always did figure there's a lot of bodies in there. You get in those woods and you can get lost. You could kill a person very easily and throw the body in there, and within three or four weeks the buzzards would have taken care of everything except the bones, and they would be scattered. The sand roads attract suicides. They use shotguns, or hoses from their exhaust pipes. In there, since 1900, there have been gangland killings, lovers'-lane killings, feud murders, and bootleggers' shoot-outs. Three years ago, a body in city clothes was found near Hampton Furnace. The case is still under investigation."

At about three o'clock, one July afternoon, in the height of the blueberry harvest, Charlie Leek, the foreman of a blueberry field, came into the Chatsworth General Store to drink a bottle of soda and to cool off. Many people in Chatsworth have small blueberry fields of their own—two to twenty-five acres. A reasonable crop picked from fifteen acres will gross ten thousand dollars. Charlie works for one of the larger growers, looking after about a hundred acres of blueberries and cranberries. I had met him at Buzby's a week or so earlier. He is a big, good-looking man with big gestures, dark hair, a weathered face, flashing blue eyes, frequent smiles, and a solid but capacious middle. He is about fifty, and he has a manner that suggests that he is not afraid to work and not afraid not to work. That day, he wore a blue shirt, dark-blue trousers, and construction worker's shoes. Sitting on the oak plank, he got into a discussion with an old man about the bread their mothers used to make. Despite the considerable difference in the two men's ages, their mothers, Charlie told me, were sisters. "This is Horace Adams, my cousin," he said. "Everybody's a relation in this burg. Yes, Horace's mother and mine used to make their own yeast, too—out of potato water and hops. Modern women aren't up to that."

"They give you cold beans," Horace Adams said. "How is the picking going, Charlie?"

"I got so disgusted I just walked away for a while," Charlie said. "I don't know where they're getting the booze, but some of them got a bucket of water out there and I bet that water is ninety proof."

Blueberry pickers in the Pine Barrens are almost all brought in from outside, but they are not migrant workers. They come mainly from Philadelphia, in privately owned school buses that bear the words "Farm Labor Transport." For the most part, the buses are driven by the men who own them, and the drivers, like their passengers, come from the city. The drivers are mainly Negroes, and so are the passengers. The drivers read newspapers and magazines all day and get three cents a pint on the berries their passengers pick. It is up to the drivers to find the pickers, and they start cruising Philadelphia streets before dawn, offering a day's work to anyone they can find, sometimes picking up men who are so drunk that they have no idea what they are getting into and who sober up in the blazing sun of the Pine Barrens wondering how they got there. Busloads vary every day. About a third of the people are steady sober pickers who make daily trips in the same bus. There are always some who do almost no work and are simply taking advantage of a chance to have a day in the country. There is usually a high percentage of schoolchildren, some of whom appear to be too young to have working papers, but at least they seem to enjoy themselves and to be there by choice. Women in their eighties ride the farm-labor transports, too. So, occasionally, do prostitutes, who go with their customers out of the blueberry clearings into the woods. Some pickers spend more in this manner than they earn during the rest of the day. Some become so drunk in the fields that they fall down in the hot sand between the blueberry bushes and pass out. "We got everything from hoochy-coochy girls on up today," Charlie told me. Pickers are paid seven cents a pint. Picking begins when the dew dries on the bushes—and is not done on rainy days—because the blue of a blueberry is a protective wax, and it comes off on the hands if the berries are wet. Some of the wax comes off anyway, and pickers' hands are always blue. A real star can earn eighteen dollars in a day, but most pickers make about ten dollars, and those who do not pick steadily make less than that. Bus drivers clear from twenty-five to fifty dollars a day. Sometimes pickers of any sort are so scarce that growers have to compete for the favor of the drivers, and on days like that the drivers have been paid as much as ninety dollars. When the pickers get into the buses and start the ride back to Philadelphia, the drivers sell them wine. On arrival in the city, some people are drunk and have spent their day's pay in the buses. (This sorry scene is not repeated during the cranberry harvest in the fall, when the bogs are flooded an inch or so over the vines, and the cranberries, which float, are batted free by motorized water rakes until they form a great scarlet berry boom—hundreds of thousands of cranberries bobbing and drifting with the wind or on a slow drainage current to a corner of the bog, where they are hauled in.)

The cultivated blueberry was developed in the Pine Barrens. More cultivated blueberries are grown there than are grown in Michigan, the No. 2 blueberry state. In 1911, Miss Elizabeth White, one of four daughters of a cranberry grower who lived about ten miles north of Chatsworth, read a publication of the United States Department of Agriculture in which a Dr. Frederick Coville described the possibilities of crossing various wild blueberries and producing superior offspring. Miss White invited Dr. Coville to use Whitesbog, her family's property, for his experiments. She gave small boards with various-sized holes in them to all pineys who were interested, and said that she would pay for blueberry bushes at a rate scaled to the size of the largest hole that the berries would not go through. Of the first hundred and twenty bushes, she and Coville threw away a hundred and eighteen. From the remaining two, they eventually made thirty-five thousand hybrid cuttings. Of the resulting bushes, they threw away all but four, from which modern cultivated blueberries, in their numerous varieties, were developed. Some of the varieties were given the names of pineys who had collected for Miss White—Grover, Rubel, Sam, Stanley, Harding, Adams, Dunfee. Miss White was in her thirties when the experiments began, and the first commercial shipments were made in 1916. In 1952, she invited landscape architects from the state highway department to Whitesbog and showed them through her blueberry fields. Miss White was over six feet tall, she carried a cane and wore a Whistler's Mother dress that was as neat as a pin. Her ankles were black from the dirt of the fields, and her hands were midnight-blue from the wax of the berries. In her home, she served each of her visitors a blueberry that was the size of a baseball, as they recall it, heaped over with sugar and resting in a pool of cream. Then she asked them to consider planting blueberry bushes along the Garden State Parkway. Miss White died a few months after that. Blueberry bushes were planted later in profusion on the margins of the parkway where it runs along the edge of the Pine Barrens.

The Rubel blueberry was named for Charlie Leek's uncle Rube Leek. The Stanley was named for Charlie's older brother. Both varieties are grown in the blueberry patch where Charlie is foreman. He told me this in his pick-up truck on the way out there from Buzby's store. He had asked me if I would like to have a look at a packing house. On the way, we went past Charlie's home, in Leektown—a settlement of six houses, five of which are occupied by people named Leek. Charlie's place is low, miscellaneously built, dark, and tarpapered. There are many fragments of machinery and several defunct vehicles in the yard. "My son Jim lives in that white house across the road from me, where I was born," he said. Looking closely, I saw traces of the white paint that had apparently covered it when Charlie was a boy.

"What did your father do?" I asked him.

"Worked in the wildwoods," he said. "Sphagnum. Wild huckleberries. Cranberries." He said that he himself had tried working outside the pines once but that he couldn't stand it and had finally come back. While he was employed at an aluminum plant on the Delaware River, he used to drink a fifth of whiskey a day, on the job. "Working with hot metal, you sweat it out," he said. "But if you drink, you abuse your family. You'll abuse your best friend, if you don't look out. I haven't had a drink since I quit that place, in 1941. It's not hard for a man to make his living here in the pines, if he ever lived here. You got wealthy men here. No one bothers you. If you don't feel good, you don't have to work. If you want to get some food, you just take your gun and go out and get it—in season. I don't outlaw. I used to. My son does a little outlawing. He has a car with a sun roof, and he and a friend hunt with it. They go through the woods and they see a deer and they stand up through the sun roof and shoot. You can do what you want to do down here. Most jobs, you have somebody breathing down your neck when you're working. Most of your natives around here aren't used to that, I can tell you that."

We had come to a clearing where thousands of blueberry bushes grew. In the center of it was the packing house—a small, low building with open and screenless windows on all sides. In front of it was a school bus marked "Farm Labor Transport." The driver stood beside his bus. He was a tall and amiable-looking man, with bare feet. He wore green trousers and a T-shirt. The end of the working day had come. Pickers were swarming around a pump—old women, middle-aged men, a young girl. A line was waiting to use an outhouse near the pump. Inside the packing house, berries half an inch thick were rolling up a portable conveyor belt and, eventually, into pint boxes. Charlie's sister was packing the boxes. Charlie's daughter-in-law was putting cellophane over them. And Charlie's son Jim was supervising the operation. Charlie picked up a pint box in which berries were mounded high, and he told me with disgust that some supermarket chains knock off these mounds of extra berries and put them in new boxes, getting three or four extra pints per twelve-box tray. At one window, pickers were turning in tickets of various colors, and they were given cash in return. One picker, who appeared to be at least in his sixties, tapped Charlie on the arm and showed him a thick packet of tickets held together with a rubber band. "I found these," the man said. "They must have fallen out of your son's pocket." He gave the packet to Charlie, who thanked him and counted the tickets.

Charlie said, "These tickets are worth seventy-five dollars."

After loading for the return trip to Philadelphia, many

buses stop in Chatsworth, so that the pickers can buy food and soft drinks at the general store. At 6 P.M. that day, they stood four and five deep all along the Buzbys' counters. One after another, they bought Coca-Cola in cold quart bottles and cookies in family-size boxes. One woman, short and middle-aged, wore a gray flannel skirt over a pair of blue-gray cotton slacks. One old man, who had swollen ankles, wore no socks, and parts of his shoes had been cut away to relieve his toes. He bought a quart of orange soda and a bag of potato chips. Half of the crowd seemed to be teen-aged. Noise was high. When the pickers had gone to their buses, Mrs. Buzby said to me, "A couple of the drivers came in here earlier to buy soda water. They use it to cut the wine."

6

The Turn of Events

In the memories of the people of Chatsworth, three local events seem to stand out in the past fifty years—the Chatsworth Fire, in 1954; the crash and death in the woods, in 1928, of an aviator who was known as Mexico's Lindbergh; and a visit, in 1927, by S.E. il Principe Constantino di Ruspoli, an authentic Italian prince who happened to be a native of Chatsworth. The Prince's father, Prince Mario Ruspoli de Poggio-Suasa—an attaché at the Italian Embassy in Washington in the eighteen-nineties—had indirectly given Chatsworth its name. During his tenure in Washington, the senior prince married an American whose family happened to own seven thousand acres of the Pine Barrens. The property was near the town of Shamong, as Chatsworth was originally called, and the Prince became so fond of the area that he and the Princess built a villa there, beside Lake Shamong, less than a mile from the middle of the town. Their son was born in the villa, and the present Mr. Buzby's mother worked as a nursemaid there. The Ruspolis entertained on the level that might be expected of a diplomat-prince. Into the pines they brought Astors, Drexels, Goulds, Armours, Morgans, Vanderbilts, the Marquise de Talleyrand-Périgord, Don Giovanni del Drago, Prince Brancaccio, and Levi P. Morton, the Vice-President of the United States. Morton (1824-1920), a Vermonter who had become a New York banker on a grand scale, was Vice-President under Benjamin Harrison and was later elected governor of New York. Like most guests of the Prince and Princess, he developed an affection for the Pine Barrens, and, with the Prince and others, he formed a syndicate that built, next to the Prince's villa, a prodigious Tudor manor house. It was three stories high, with oak half timbers, brooding gables, and five huge chimneys. This new phenomenon in the pines was named the Chatsworth Country Club—after Chatsworth House, the country seat of the Duke of Devonshire, a friend of various members of the syndicate. Before long, the piney colliers and sawyers of Shamong agreed to change the name of the town itself to Chatsworth and the name of the lake to Chatsworth Lake. The Chatsworth Country Club had seven hundred members around the turn of the century, but its era was to be a short one. When the Prince was sent by his government to another country, the woodland retreat lost much of its appeal. By 1912, an Italian real-estate firm was trying—with no success—to promote it as an attraction for Italian tourists in the United States. Buzby has a pamphlet, published in Italian, that speaks stirringly of the great hall and of the Prince's splendid *palazzina* beside it, in a setting where the air is forever *profumata*

§ 98 §

with the scent of a million pines. The villa and the manor house stood empty for many years and slowly disintegrated. Draperies hung in place for decades and gradually moldered. Red silk that covered the walls fell away in strips. When the native prince came to Chatsworth to see his birthplace, that is how it appeared to him. He spent one afternoon in the town. He is now dead. Nothing whatever remains of the Chatsworth Country Club—not even a discernible trace of its outlines—and where the villa stood the only remnants are a few scattered bricks.

Near the headwaters of Tulpehocken Creek is a small clearing where a monument stands, twelve feet high, made of cement in the shape of a pylon. There are two tall flagpoles near it. Out there in one of the wildest parts of the Pine Barrens, trees have been cleared to make three crescent-shaped parking lots behind the monument, although the road that runs by it is untravelled for hours and sometimes days at a time. An Aztec falling eagle stands out in relief on one side of the monument, and Spanish words spill down another, in memory of *"capitan aviador Emilio Carranza, muerto tragicamente el 13 de julio 1928."* Carranza was twenty-three when he died. He had been a Mexican hero since he was eighteen, when he strafed Yaqui Indians in Sonora while helping to put down the de la Huerta rebellion. Once, one of his wings caught fire and he flew into a thunderhead, where rain put out the flames. His hair was parted in the middle, and he had a long, thin, sad face, more Andalusian than Mexican. After a crash in Sonora, his face bones were set with platinum screws. He was a great-nephew of President Venustiano Carranza, who was assassinated in 1920. With the Carranza name and his military honors, he was the logical choice of the Mexican government to make a good-will flight, in 1928, from Mexico City non-stop to Washington. This was a formal response to a good-will flight made in the reverse direction by Charles Lindbergh the previous December. Carranza, who took off on June 11, 1928, flew a Ryan monoplane, as Lindbergh did, and newspapers called him "Mexico's Lone Eagle." Fog overcame Carranza in Mooresville, North Carolina, and his non-stop flight to Washington included a stop there until the fog lifted. This detail was politely deëmphasized in the warm flurry of inter-presidential telegrams that celebrated his trip, and in the speeches and parades that welcomed him to Washington and, later, New York. His heroism was acknowledged by Secretary of Commerce Herbert Hoover and Mayor Jimmy Walker. Nonetheless, he had failed to carry out his mission as planned, and he intended to redress the failure by flying home non-stop from New York to Mexico City. Getting away from newsmen, he left Manhattan earlier than he had said he would, and went out to Roosevelt Field on Long Island on July 13th. It was a day of thunderstorms. He waited for one to let up, then took off and headed south before another one closed in. There was, however, a thunderstorm over the Pine Barrens, and it apparently killed him. People in Chatsworth still stand around in the general store and say they heard a plane in difficulty in the sky that day, and some say they heard it crash, but no search party went out, and it is unlikely that the crash or even the sound of the plane—in the rumbling thunder —was ever heard at all. Henry Carr, of Chatsworth, and his wife, Marie, were out gathering wild blueberries a couple of days later and came upon the wreckage—at the site of the present memorial, in Tabernacle Township, six miles from Chatsworth. "The men who went out and got him brought Carranza over to our garage and put him on Mother's ironing board," Buzby tells people. A few days later, a thirty-two-gun salute was fired on the front steps of Pennsylvania Station as the body left New York by rail for Mexico City, where three hundred thousand people followed Carranza's cortege to the Dolores Cemetery.

On a Saturday in July, an annual ceremony is held at the graveside in Mexico, and at the same time a ceremony is held in the Pine Barrens at the Carranza Memorial. I was present a summer ago, on an overwhelmingly hot day with a cloudless sky. Three hundred people were there, half of them Mexican. The Mexicans came from as far away as Chicago, but most of them were from New York, northern New Jersey, or Pennsylvania. They were in costume, in the main, and before the ceremony began they played strident arrangements of Mexican songs, like "Mi Patria Es Lo Primero" and "Mi Lindo Monterrey," on a record-player that was set on the tailgate of a Chevrolet station wagon. Girls in florid skirts and white blouses took thirty minutes to make up, combing and spraying one another's hair and swaying to the sound of the phonograph. Little boys wore frilled shirts and straw hats. One man wore a green-white-and-orange sombrero, a red bandanna around his neck, and a black shirt. A Mexican colonel, tall and trim in a deep-green uniform, walked through the crowd and took a seat in a folding chair under a canopy, where people from Chatsworth and other places in the pines sat quietly in the heat, waiting. Two trucks from the state Forest Fire Service arrived, a bus and a truck from Fort Dix, and an ambulance. A fire warden came out of the woods carrying a six-foot pine snake. Mexican children formed a circle around him, and he told them that a group of Boy Scouts had cut the head off a rattlesnake in that same part of the woods three days before. An Army band from Fort Dix put the Mexican phonograph to shame with a soft and beautiful flow of Mexican melodies, notably "La Paloma" and the "Zacatecas March." There were thirty-five men in the band, including a blond soldier with a bowl haircut who had the touch of Granada with a pair of castanets. American Legionnaires with red-veined, waxy faces walked around saying, "Where's the beer?" The beer was on ice in a large blue garbage can under a pitch pine, and the Legionnaires—who came from the Mt. Holly area, outside the pines—shared it with the Tabernacle Township police, one of whom was so heavy that he could not reach down into the garbage can. Brigadier General William C. Doyle, of Fort Dix, gave an address, and said, "Here in New Jersey's pine country, the gallant airman was grounded forever. He was not dess-tined to complete his mission." The Honorable Donald E. Johnson, Imme-

diate Past National Commander of the American Legion, said in the course of his speech that he had recently spent "an unprecedented hour with the President of Mexico." He also spoke about the war in Vietnam, saying, "Anyone who tells you this is a civil war is either ill-informed or uninformed or deliberately deceptive." There was no discernible reaction from either the Mexicans or the pineys. Finally, he mentioned Emilio Carranza, saying, "Had Captain Carranza lived, his name might be forgotten today—such are the imponderables of life and death." Another Legionnaire informed the crowd that men of the American Legion had hacked a trail twenty-five miles through the wilderness to carry Carranza's body out to Mt. Holly. Actually, Carranza crashed beside a sand road, and his body was removed easily to Chatsworth. What the Mt. Holly Legionnaires have done, though, is to organize and maintain the annual ceremony. Ten large floral wreaths were placed around the memorial. Six United States soldiers raised rifles, a second lieutenant said, "Sergeant of the firing squad, prepare to salute the dead," and three rounds were fired. A soldier played "Taps." From the two flagpoles, the flags of Mexico and the United States descended. There was a contrail fifty thousand feet above this scene, and at a lower altitude a Navy jet fighter passed over it as well. A young man named Antonio Huitron, who had a child in his arms, and who lived on 176th Street in New York and had been in the United States for six years, said to me at this moment, "It was very sad, because everyone in Mexico was expecting him to come back."

Three or four days after the ceremony, I went again to the memorial, this time with Fred Brown. The wreaths, which were on stands, had fallen over in a wind. All papers, cups, and beer cans had been taken away, and the memorial clearing, wreaths aside, looked just as it had when I first saw it—desolate and improbable. "I heard him," Fred said. "I heard him when he went down. That was in an awful thunderstorm. I heard him circling. I said to my wife, 'There's an airplane in trouble.' Then I didn't hear it no more. I knew from the sound that it was out in the Hocken Lowlands where he crashed. I come out here the next day. This was tall timber here. It's burnt since he went down." Fred walked to a large pine that had been left standing in the cleared area, and he paced out four yards from the tree. "Carranza's wing fell three hundred yards up that way," he said, gesturing to the east. "The rest of the airplane hit this tree, and right here is where his head was. There wasn't no blood where he laid. What do you suppose—he just bled inside? There was no blood. He had a flashlight still in his hand, an ordinary nickel flashlight, no more than a two-cell." Carranza's widow visited Chatsworth some years after her husband's death. She wore a purple blouse and a purple skirt, and protruding from her sandals were purple toenails. Carranza's sister also came. She flew over the monument and scattered roses from the air. The road that leads into the pines through Tabernacle Township and goes past the memorial and on to Speedwell is not marked with a name, even on topographic maps. For al-

most thirty years, however, the people of the Pine Barrens have called it Carranza's Road.

The lookout watcher in the fire tower on Apple Pie Hill,
which is about three miles north of Carranza's Road and
three miles west of Chatsworth, is a man named Eddie
Parker. He has held the job for twenty-four years, man-
ning the tower when the woods are dry, and he finds it
disagreeably lonely. He does not use a particular tech-
nique, such as a grid system for periodic checking. Day
after day, he just watches the woods. He can see hundreds of square miles of the pinelands, but even small
amounts of smoke will quickly attract his eyes. "If a fire
starts, it is like someone put a new chair in my living
room," he explains to people who visit his tower. "I see
it right away." He has seen a lot of fires, for the Pine
Barrens are particularly flammable, as woodlands go, and
they are the scene of some of the most spectacular forest
fires that occur in the United States.

July 12, 1954, was a hot day in a time of drought. The
woods of the greater Chatsworth area were "loaded with
fuel," as foresters put it, for there had been no large fires
in that section for some years. The Chatsworth Fire, as
it eventually came to be known, started in a cedar swamp
nine miles southwest of the town. Eddie Parker saw it at
4:04 P.M. and called it in. In a short time, twenty-five
men had reached the cedar swamp. They had back tanks
and other portable equipment, and also three four-wheel-
drive trucks carrying two-hundred-gallon water tanks.
When the men arrived, only three acres had burned. At

7:30 P.M., they reported the fire under control. The ground was so dry, however, that the fire was burning down into the turf of the swamp. By morning, it had spread over about twelve acres, and had gone so deep that it could not be put out. It was surrounded by firefighters, but sometime in the forenoon of July 13th it escaped. The flames began to move east before brisk winds. The strategy and number of the firefighters had to expand with the fire. By 3 P.M., fire lines were being plowed and backfires set in an effort to contain the destruction within an area of six hundred acres. Winds grew in force and began to shift. Spot fires from flying embers appeared all over the woods downwind. By midnight, new lines had been established and the new area of containment was five thousand acres. A forest fire moves in a V, like the wake of a ship. The point of the V is called the head fire, and if it gets up into the tops of the trees it is also called a crówn fire. The sides of the V, which burn slowly outward, are called lateral fires, and they have to be fought by men with back tanks and shovels, for if lateral fires get far enough out to catch a wind of their own with fresh fuel in front of them, they can become new head fires. At 8 A.M. on July 14th, a fire warden named William Phoenix flew over the fire in a light plane and reported that it seemed to be pretty much under control. That afternoon, however, winds even higher than those of the two previous days came up, and, before them, several new head fires developed, in broadly separated places. These new head fires jumped the previous lines of containment. They crowned, and, like warships converging, they moved toward Chatsworth. By this time, some two hundred fire trucks had come from all over central and southern New Jersey, and even from Pennsylvania. The United States Army had arrived. Many women in Chatsworth packed what they could and left the town. People buried things. A man who lived in the woods north of Chatsworth buried his refrigerator.

"The whole earth was burning up," Mrs. Buzby said. "Everybody thought the town was going to be burned out. The fire jumped the lake. You could see nothing but dense smoke. The sand was burned black. The wind was terrific. Fire creates wind, you know. The sky overhead was all afire. A piece of the roof of the Coopers' house blew off, burning, and went a quarter of a mile through the air. It landed on a house and burned it up. Everybody thought the world was coming to an end, I guess. It looked like the heavens had lit up. We were all scared to death. We were all praying pretty hard. After the fire jumped through the town one time, the wind shifted and it started to come back. They say that a fire can't go back over ground it has already crossed, but this one did. A neighbor and I stood here on the steps of the store and watched. 'The town's going,' she said. 'Let's go for the lake.' I said, 'No, I'm going to stick.' "

By nightfall, the winds were moving at seventy miles an hour, and Chatsworth did seem to be doomed. Sparks from the returning fire were actually showering into the streets when rain began to fall. A brief but extremely heavy rainstorm drenched Chatsworth. People who watched the fire from distant hills say that the storm moved across the woods like a dark, reaching arm and, coming to the reddest part of the fire, killed it. Segments burned on for three weeks more, but most of the destruction had been ended by the storm over Chatsworth, which saved the town. Twelve buildings were burned, and nineteen thousand five hundred acres of land.

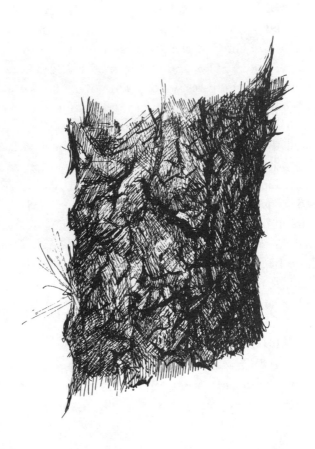

7

Fire in the Pines

W<small>HATEVER ELSE THEY DO, MEN IN THE</small>
Pine Barrens are firefighters throughout their lives. There
are about four hundred forest fires in the pinelands
every year, and fifteen or twenty of them are major
ones (more than a hundred acres). It has been theorized
that the pineys are defeatists because of the constant
presence of the danger of fire. They are, at any rate,
extremely fire-conscious, and they know what to expect
of a fire when one moves through the woods. Head fires
can be as little as ten feet deep. A person overtaken by
a head fire can turn, go through it, and get onto safe,
burned ground. One of the first lessons in forest-fire
survival is: Get onto burned ground. But this is not always easy. Head fires can also be as much as half a mile
deep. Lateral fires can be only a foot deep, but they can
also be a hundred feet deep. In 1936, a cousin of the fire
watcher Eddie Parker was caught in the middle when
a head fire and a backfire came together. He had no
time to get to burned ground. The last living thing he
did was to kneel, as he burned, and embrace a pine tree.

Some fires are hotter than others. What makes the difference between a standard blaze and an inferno is something called fuel continuity. This is the ladderlike arrangement of litter, understory, and overstory that naturally builds up, with time, in the forest. It begins with leaves and pine needles and other litter on the forest floor, moves up to sheep laurel and blueberries and huckleberries, on up to scrub oaks and laurel and young pines, on up to trees of intermediate age, and finally to the crowns of the tallest trees. In order to remove the lower part of this ladder, the litter and the understory may be burned under control in winter, and where this has been done the results have been dramatic. Wildfires have raced through the forest and, upon reaching control-burned areas, have stopped dead. Unfortunately, there is not manpower enough to do a really significant amount of controlled burning. As much is done in Wharton State Forest as anywhere, and of its ninety-six thousand acres only about seven thousand are control-burned each winter. Wildfires have burned more than a third of the Wharton Forest since 1954.

"I like fire. I like to fight fire," the chief Wharton forester, Sydney Walker, said to me one day. "Fire is the key down here." Equipment is, to a considerable extent, mechanical now. Hand fighting with shovels and rakes has largely been supplanted by the use of tractor-drawn plows to cut forty-eight-inch swaths through the woods, along which backfires are set with kerosene torches. The big water trucks, some of which can hold five hundred gallons, are making back tanks obsolete. Aerial techniques are improving steadily. Airdrops, from light planes, used to be made with volclay, a fine clay mixed with water. Well placed, a clay airdrop could retard a fire. Now, liquid fertilizer (nitrogen and phosphorus, one to three) has replaced volclay, and when the fertilizer hits in the right place it will smother a modest fire altogether. Airdrops require skillful and nervy flying. About a hundred and eighty gallons of mixture are laid down, necessarily from a low altitude, and the target is the head fire. Done properly, a drop will cover an area of about a half acre. Pilots with experience in combat sometimes lack whatever it is that will make a man run a slow plane in close over a crown fire. A typical report of the Forest Fire Service in such a case said, "The pilot was a retired Air Force lieutenant colonel with no previous experience in fire-bombing. Although he was repeatedly advised that it was of major importance that we get to the fire swiftly before it could build up, he took an inordinately long time in takeoff. His helmet and goggles took a long time to adjust and he appeared slower than other pilots in starting his motor. Although his pilot's reports show from fifty to one hundred feet as being the height from which he dropped his load of retardant, the ground crew in general reported that he was much higher. One warden remarked, 'He will never put out any fire dropping from that height.' And another warden said, 'He was so high he looked like a sparrow.'"

Fire in the pines is never spontaneous, and lightning sets only about one per cent. There is an area in the

northeastern part of the woods where most of the lightning fires begin, probably because there is a concentra-
tion of iron deposits there. It is supposed that the Chatsworth Fire started when a cigarette was tossed away by
one of a group of woodcutters who were clearing the
cedar swamp where the fire began. Carelessness is the
cause of many fires, but not to the overwhelming extent that one might imagine. A remarkably common
cause of fire in the pines is arson. Standing in all that
dry sand, the forests glisten with oils and resins that—
to some people—seem to beg for flame. Oak leaves in
forests that are damp and rich are different from Pine
Barrens oak leaves, which have so much protective oil
concentrated within them that they appear to be made
of shining green leather. The ground soaks up rainfall
so efficiently that the litter on its surface is, more often
than not, as dry as paper. In the sand soil, there are no
earthworms and few bacteria to consume the litter, and
it piles up three and four inches deep. In all, the Pine
Barrens respond explosively to flame, and thus they appear to be irresistible to incendiaries of many kinds. Of
the thirty-seven fires that occurred in the Wharton
Forest in 1966, for example, the foresters say that
twenty-four were definitely set by arsonists and three
others probably were. The year before that, elsewhere
in the pines, one man alone set sixty-nine fires. He was,
at the time, a policeman in a town on the edge of the
woods. After his actions became known, he was described by surprised neighbors as "a good family man"
and "a nice guy." He himself "discovered" and reported

all sixty-nine fires, usually calling them in on the police radio, and when he had been placed under arrest he couldn't explain why he had felt compelled to set the woods ablaze. Another man, in recent years, stole an arm patch from a fire warden and turned up at forest fires as a participant in the fighting. Wherever he was working, spot fires would break out, until the pattern of coincidences entangled him. After a fire, men from the Forest Fire Service go through the area where the burning began, often on their hands and knees, sifting through the ashes for evidence of the cause. Sometimes they find bits of railroad flares. More often, they find the remains of an ordinary matchbook with a wire wrapped around it. Incendiaries use the wire to add weight to the matchbook so that it will carry some distance into the woods when they toss it flaming from their automobiles. That way, they don't have to get out and walk. Almost without exception, arson in the pines is committed by people who come in from the outside. Pineys *have* set grudge fires from time to time, and colliers used to set fires because charred wood was good only for charcoal and they could buy it cheaply from the owners of the burned land. Pineys also used to make "skeeter smoke" by burning a mixture of pine needles, pine cones, pine chips, and charcoal in pans on their stoves. The smoke permeated their houses, and mosquitoes stayed away. Sometimes these smudge fires jumped off the stoves, burned down houses, and expanded into forest fires. Years ago, the pineys deliberately set fires in blueberry lowlands, because wild blueberry bushes will come back strong after a fire and produce more berries than they yielded before. This practice is still carried on by gatherers of wild blueberries in Maine, Vermont, and New Hampshire, but is forbidden in the Pine Barrens, where it was once given as the cause of a tenth of all forest fires. A relatively new cause of fire in the pines is burning automobiles. Foresters make their way through the smoldering aftermath of a headlong fire and at the source they find a blackened automobile. Teen-age hoods steal cars in cities, take them into the pines, strip them, ignite them, and leave the scene.

The Forest Fire Service has indices that show when the woods are least and most vulnerable to fire. There may be fires almost any day of the spring, summer, and fall, but when the indices are high the fires tend to be big. First, there is something called the buildup index, which takes into account the ground moisture and also whether the vegetation is cured, transitional, or green. When wind velocities, barometric readings, and fuel-moisture levels are added in, the result is the burning index. The scale of the burning index goes from zero to two hundred. On April 20, 1963, the day of the worst forest fire in the recorded history of the Pine Barrens, the burning index shot past two hundred into the indeterminable beyond. It was not a particularly hot day, but the vegetation was still in the cured stage, winds were blowing at about fifty miles an hour, and there was a drought. Once a fire got started, there was not much chance that it could be controlled. Actually, twelve non-contiguous major fires started on that day. The big one began after a man who was burning brush about seven miles west of Mt. Misery left his fire because he thought it was out. It was brought under control about thirty miles to the east at midnight on April 23rd, and it was finally pronounced out on May 1st. Smoke from this fire palled the air and deeply reddened the sun as far away as Princeton. The men who fought the fire made stand after stand—first at a state highway and later at county roads, sand roads, and plowed lines—only to have the flames burst over them and force them to regroup farther east. Embers went into the upper winds and advanced as much as two miles at a jump, starting new fires where they landed. Several crown fires were spread out over a six-mile front, and rolling white heat was trailed by streaks of orange flame. The fire was so hot that it caused the surfaces of macadam roads to form bubbles. Overhead, white piles of smoke went up hundreds of feet, and against this white background, now and again, appeared black twisters of smoke from pitch. Multiple airdrops were made but did not significantly help. Finally, the crews were forced back all the way to the Garden State Parkway, where, forming long lines and working with shovels and back tanks, they made a last try to control the fire. They held it there, but it had only a few miles to go anyway before it would have reached the sea. One man died. As in the Chatsworth Fire, the damage to buildings was relatively light, but only because there were so few buildings to damage. The fire crossed the Pine Barrens from one side to the other, and burned seventy-five thousand nine hundred and twenty-five acres.

A color photograph taken of a section of woods just after the 1963 fire shows about what you would expect —blackened spars above a smoldering forest floor. A photograph taken from the same spot two months later presents to the viewer a forest panoply of summer green. Of all the natural phenomena of the Pine Barrens, the most startling one is the speed with which the vegetation comes back from fire. There has been so much fire in the pines for so many centuries that, through the resulting processes of natural selection, the species that grow there are not only highly flammable but are able to tolerate fire and come back quickly. There are only three kinds of pines in the United States that respond to fires by putting forth sprouts. Two of these—the pitch pine and the short-leaf pine—predominate in the Pine Barrens. (The other, the Chihuahua pine, grows in New Mexico.) The sprouts develop from dormant buds in the trunks and larger limbs, and soon after the fire dies down, out they come. All over the woods are pine trees with splendid green crowns and trunks that are still black from old fires. Oaks that are burned usually die at the top, but they reshoot from the roots. Chestnut oaks put out so many sprouts all around their trunks that in time the shoots form palisaded enclosures resembling jails, and drunken pineys were once incarcerated in them and left there until they sobered up. Almost every woody species in the Pine Barrens has the ability to sprout after fire. The understory starts right up again, and bracken fern and sheep laurel are particularly fast. Scrub oaks put out so many acorns after a fire that they look like over-decorated Christmas trees. This helps to increase, among other things, the communities of deer and grouse.

It is because of fire that pines are predominant in the Pine Barrens. There is thought to be a progression in the development of any forest from pioneer species to climax trees. Most ecologists agree that if fire were kept out of the Pine Barrens altogether, the woods would eventually be dominated by a climax of black oaks, white oaks, chestnut oaks, scarlet oaks, and a lesser proportion of hickories and red maples. In some areas, oaks dominate now. Fire, however, has generally stopped the march of natural progression, and the resulting situation is one that might be called biological inertia—apparently endless cycles of fire and sprouting. Fire favors the pine trees because they have thick bark that provides insulation from high temperatures, and also because burned ground is just about perfect for pine seedbeds. Oaks lose vigor when they are repeatedly burned. They develop heart rot, and they die. Scarlet oaks go first, then chestnut oaks, then white oaks, then black oaks. Blackjack oaks are an exception and after a fire come back strong. In an area where a fire has been extremely hot, the pines die and the blackjack oaks put out basal sprouts that grow to be the predominant trees in that section. But, for the most part, fires are not that intense, and, working in behalf of the pitch and shortleaf pines, they clear out the competition. It would be an error, however, to think of forest fires as magic wands that clean the woods. Controlled burning can have this effect, but wildfires leave an ugly trail. Oak spars and—if the fire was hot enough—pine spars stick up everywhere. There are sprouts, but for a time there is no shade. Even when pines develop new crowns, several seasons must go by before the crowns are full. The white cedars, which are the most beautiful trees in the Pine Barrens, are killed outright if they are burned, and for years—standing feathery and dead—they commemorate the wildfire that took them. Foresters can cut an old pine and read in its occasional dark rings the dates of fires that have gone through the area in which it stands; 1930, 1927, 1924, 1922, 1916, 1910, 1905, 1894, 1885, and 1872 are the dates of dark rings that can still be read in some trees. Causes differed, but fires were frequent in the pines in the eighteenth and seventeenth centuries, and before that Indians burned the woods to improve conditions for hunting and travel. Almost certainly, the role of fire in the development of the Pine Barrens has been of importance since post-Wisconsin time, when the patterns of the present vegetation began to form as the great Wisconsin ice sheet receded.

The glacier reached only about as far south as Morristown, which is fifty miles north of the pines, but the torrents that poured from it as it melted carried southward prodigious loads of gravel that mounded here and there into what are now some of the hills of the Pine Barrens. As the early vegetation developed, the climate of the area was still arctic. The Pine Barrens were then a cold desert of permafrost and tundra—a scene that I found myself imagining at one point while I was spending some time with three men from the National Park Service who were making a general survey of the pinelands area. One man had recently returned from two years in Alaska. Standing on the observation platform of the fire tower on Bear Swamp Hill, he remarked that the Pine Barrens reminded him very much of Alaska, going on to say that the evergreen species were different but that their general appearance—and the appearance of the undulating land—was much the same from that high perspective. There is a theory that the Hudson River once flowed much farther south than it does now, and that it passed through the Pine Barrens, leaving more gravels, which eventually became more hills. Helderberg limestone from the upper Hudson Valley is found in the pines. When white men first saw the region, many of the pitch and shortleaf pines were about two hundred years old and about twenty inches in diameter. The white cedars, in their swamps, were larger. Some of them were six feet thick at the base and a thousand years old. When these great trees fell, some of them sank beneath the sphagnum moss and deep into the swamps, where they were sealed away from oxygen and were also protected from fungi by the acidulous muck. They were thus preserved. The mining of ancient cedar logs was once a source of income to some people in the pines, and even today the logs are occasionally found and removed. From them come the most durable of all cedar boards and shingles. During the Second World War, wood from sunken cedar logs taken from Pine Barrens swamps was used in the hulls of patrol torpedo boats. In Lebanon State Forest, which is four miles north of Chatsworth, foresters have put on display a pair of mined cedar logs, each about four feet thick.

No one has yet determined with certainty how the dwarf forests of the eastern Pine Barrens developed, but there have been many hypotheses, and, as one after another has been shown to be unsound, the process of elimination has led back to fire. Frequent as fires are everywhere in the pines, they are more frequent in the dwarf forests than anywhere else. The dwarf forests occur in two upland areas, which do not quite touch one another. The Upper Plains and the Lower Plains, as they are called, cover about twenty thousand acres. Pitch pines predominate there, as they do elsewhere in the Pine Barrens, but instead of rising fifty or sixty feet into the air they rise five feet. A snapshot of the Plains will often seem to take in huge expanses of forest, as if the picture had been made from a low-flying airplane, unless a human being happens to have been standing in the camera's range, in which case the person's head seems almost grotesque and planetary, outlined in sky above the tops of the trees. There is aluminum in the soil of the Plains, and one prominent hypothesis was that aluminum toxicity stunts the trees. Equal amounts of aluminum have been found, however, in Pine Barrens soils where trees grow high. Another hypothesis, long in vogue among botanists and soil scientists, was that a layer of hardpan a short distance beneath the surface was stunting the vegetation. But a graduate student from Rutgers dug three hundred well-spaced holes a few years ago and concluded that there is little or no hardpan under the Plains. Because the Plains are on high ground and winds are fierce there, it has been thought that the little trees are wind-stunted. But the Plains are not on the highest ground in the Pine Barrens. Winds are at least as fierce on the higher ground elsewhere, and the trees there are of normal height. According to the Nantucket-tip-moth theory, a small creature in the Plains eats into the pine trees' terminal shoots and cuts them back, dwarfing the trees. The tip moth, however, does not eat oaks, and twenty-two per cent of the trees in the Plains are oaks and they are just as tiny as the pines. Fred Brown gave me his own explanation for the existence of the Plains when we went there one day. "This ground is so poor a pismire can't live on it," he said. "If you found a pismire here, he'd be half starved to death." Studies have shown that the soil of the Plains is about the same as the soil of the rest of the Pine Barrens. What remains is fire. Wildfires have completely swept the Plains on an average of once every seven years for centuries. Young trees there that have not yet been hit by fire are apparently normal and have taproots, but after the trees have burned they lose their taproots, and their lateral roots spread abnormally far out—from twenty to thirty feet—forming a great mat with the lateral roots of other trees, all of which are dwarfs. The correlation with fire is apparent, but no one can say how fire causes the stunting. Another curiosity apparently brought about by fire is the type of pine cone that develops in the Plains. There are two races of pitch pines. One race has open cones (these are the familiar pine cones that have gaps between their scales) and the other race has closed cones (the scales fit tightly together, and the surfaces of the cones are smooth). Open cones drop from the trees once a year, but closed cones hang on until a fire comes, or until so many years have passed that they are finally squeezed off by other cones. In either case, aloft or on the ground, closed cones remain closed until they are opened by fire. Taxonomically, the open-cone race and the closed-cone race are not distinguished. In the Pine Barrens outside the Plains, the great majority of the pitch pines are of the open-cone race. In the Plains, ninety-nine per cent of the dwarf pitch pines produce closed cones. This, again, does not indicate why the trees are stunted, but it seems to point to the exceptional frequency of fire in the Plains, where the closed-cone race has been selected. Jack McCormick, who is chairman of the Department of Ecology and Land Management at the Academy of Natural Sciences of Philadelphia, spent an afternoon with me in the Plains, where he explained these hypotheses and phenomena. His doctoral dissertation was a study of two watersheds elsewhere in the Pine Barrens, and when he was working on it he lived in a trailer in the woods for two years. He feels that the Plains are ecologically unique, and he says that they are somewhat analogous to the chaparral of southern California. He hopes that the Plains will be left as they are. "From studies made here, we can add to our fund of information about the behavior of species under the influence of fire," he said. "Heaven knows what we'll find out. The average frequency of fires—once every six or seven years—means nothing in itself. Rapid sequence of fires—say, when three occur in six years—may have something to do with dwarfism. Also, at least to my knowledge, no one has planted an open-cone pitch pine and a closed-cone pitch pine side by side to see what would happen. Nor has anyone cross-pollinated open- and closed-cone pines. We don't know which is dominant. We don't know what a hybrid would do. We don't know a God-damned thing."

Near Warren Grove, in the Lower Plains, the Navy has a target area for skip bombers and dive bombers. The planes dive soundlessly, like toys on strings, all but hitting the five-foot trees as they pull out of their dives and simultaneously drop their payloads in the target area, usually with a concerted accuracy—plane after plane after plane—that is almost unbelievable. After each plane has gone and is moving up into the sky as if it were on the inside rim of a wheel, the sound of its jet comes to a ground observer—much too late to be connected in any sensible way with its source. Three years ago, one pilot did not pull out of a dive, and his exploding plane started a major forest fire.

8

The Fox Handles the Day

Twenty-three kinds of orchids grow in the Pine Barrens—including the green wood orchid, the yellow-crested orchid, the white-fringed orchid, the white arethusa, the rose pogonia, and the helleborine—and they are only the beginning of a floral wherewithal that botanists deeply fear they will some-day lose. One day, I heard a lady botanist say, with gentle anguish in her voice, "If Sim Place were developed, what would happen to *Habenaria integra* then?" *Habenaria integra*, the yellow southern fringe-less orchid, grows mainly around Sim Place, a semi-ghost town several miles east of Hog Wallow. The people the lady was addressing could, of course, give no answer; they simply looked more or less distressed. The occasion was a summer field trip of the Philadelphia Botanical Club, on a day so debilitatingly hot that only a loyal core of about a dozen people had met at a Pine Barrens crossroads and proceeded as planned through several areas of woods. Six hundred and fifty thousand acres of wilderness were spread out around them, but they moved virtually on tiptoe to avoid hurting plants underfoot. One of the first species they examined was the threadleaved sundew, which grows in boggy depressions and, like several Pine Barrens plants, is insectivorous. There is little nitrogen in Pine Barrens soil, and the region has selected some plant species that get their nitrogen elsewhere—mainly from the bodies of insects. The filiform leaves of the sundews were spread out like the spines of umbrellas, and their glands were covered with a glutinous secretion that sparkled in the sun. Brooks Evert, an insurance executive, whose wife had organized the outing, carefully scooped up a sundew in a large handful of the wet sand it was growing in. He showed it to the group. Caught in the shining fluid on the sundew's glands, several winged creatures were struggling and dying. Evert carefully set the plant back in the ground as he had found it. Mrs. Evert said, "As a rule, we take nothing and we leave nothing." The group moved onward through the bog, passing thousands of additional sundews. "Oh, my goodness," another woman said. "I'm stepping on them."

In the group were, among others, a physician, a horticulturist, a management consultant, and, most notably, Edgar T. Wherry, professor emeritus of botany at the University of Pennsylvania. Wherry is the author of *The Wild Flower Guide* and *The Fern Guide*, each work the standard of its field, and he also developed the method that is used today to test the alkalinity and acidity of soil. He is a tall man in his eighties, quite thin and frail-looking. When someone, greeting him, asked him how he was, he said, "Still around, somehow." Even when he spoke, he seldom looked at anything but the ground, in his search for specimens that might be of particular interest to the others. He wore a green eyeshade. He seemed to care a little less than some of the others for the life-span of an individual plant, and he also seemed less respectful of Latinate, scientific names. "This is candy root," he said, pulling a plant out of the ground. "Taste it." The root of the plant had the taste of a sweet peppermint candy cane. "I like regular names better than scientific names—they don't mean anything to people," Wherry went on. "When I got up a book on wild flowers, I tried to find the colloquial names, if any, rather than the scientific names."

"What is this, Dr. Wherry?" someone asked him, pointing to a small plant with greenish-white leaves.

"Dogbane," he said. "Why 'dogbane' no one knows. I never saw a dog pay any attention to it."

Asked what plants in the Pine Barrens are botanically most important, Wherry said that the curly-grass fern, which was discovered there and grows almost nowhere else, is in a class by itself. "After that, there are several plants of special interest," he went on. "*Narthecium*, the bog asphodel, is isolated here. It's disjunct. You don't see it again until you get to the North Carolina mountains. Goldcrest grows here, too, and its nearest relative is in Australia. *Lycopodium carolinianum*, the slender club moss, ranges from the Pine Barrens to Florida, then jumps to South Africa. Any plant that is able to do that has a great geological history. To me, that's one of the most remarkable ranges of all the plants that are here." The group found and examined the curly-grass fern, bog asphodel, and club moss. Wherry pulled up another kind of moss and pointed out its spores, saying, "This is foxtail moss. The spores are explosive. The Chinese used them for gunpowder." He showed the group mountain mint and cat briar. "Cat-briar shoots are tender and taste like fresh peas or asparagus," he said. "Deer like cat briar."

Mrs. Evert called out to her husband, "Brooks, keep your eyes open and see if you can see the adder's-tongue fern over there." Someone else found an adder's-tongue fern, and all the others assembled around it, on their hands and knees, as they did, moments later, around an orchid called Loesel's twayblade. This was in Martha, and the orchid was growing on the site of the mansion that had stood in the middle of the now vanished town. Overhead, crowded down by the pines, were the strangely twisted catalpa trees that had been planted by the people of Martha in the first half of the nineteenth century.

"The catalpa trees sure don't look happy," said one woman.

"They are weeds of civilization," said Wherry. "So is ebony spleenwort," he added, and he pulled up an ebony spleenwort, which is a small fern, and explained that it is not native to the Pine Barrens, nor could it be, because the soil there is too acid for it. Wherever man has used lime to build structures, however, ebony spleen-wort can be found. Spores come in on the wind from heaven knows what distances. Often this alien plant is the only existing sign that a house—or a town—once stood where it grows. Ebony spleenwort is found in abundance around the building sites in all the vanished towns, but it is found nowhere else in the pines. Wherry moved on to a patch of velvet grass and said that it was "another invader as a result of man's activities." He also said that there is no poison ivy in the Pine Barrens except where man has made clearings and disturbed the earth.

Leading the group into wide bogs that were once Martha Pond, Mrs. Evert said, "Come look for *Utricularia resupinata*. The best way to find it is to squat. Then you're on your own." Everyone squatted on his own. A lady in a blue hat, a blue blouse, blue slacks, and blue sneakers found a pink orchid (*Calopogon pulchellus*) instead.

"Would anyone like my lens?" Mrs. Evert said. Through her lens, the orchid appeared to be made of crystal foam covered with patches of purple glazing.

The sphagnum surface of the bogs seemed to quake. Wherry said that in the United States quaking bogs are almost unique to the Pine Barrens—that there are some quaking bogs in the pinelands of North Carolina, but they are dry and firm in summer. He added that the flora of the pinelands of New Jersey and North Carolina "are related but not identical in any sense."

"When you spend a day in these bogs, it's a good idea to bring a change of feet," Mrs. Evert said.

Wherry pointed out rattlesnake ferns, cinnamon ferns, papery bluish-gray marsh ferns, bold and lacy royal ferns. Before the outing was over, the group had found Indian shoestrings, Turk's-cap lilies, some rare spreading pogonias, swamp azaleas, swamp hyacinths, wild magnolias, cassandras, and prickly pears—the only cactus that is native east of the Mississippi River. Walking out of the woods at the end, Wherry said, "To have all this destroyed by a jetport, or by anything else, would be an ecological disaster."

I once met a man from the New Jersey state geologist's office, in Trenton, who has made hundreds of trips through the Pine Barrens. He told me that one of the most remarkable things about the region is that the great silence there is not broken by so much as a bird-call, since the pines are so barren that there is nothing for birds to eat. That one ranks high in the large catalogue of misconceptions that people elsewhere in New Jersey have about the Pine Barrens, for the trees there are full of noisy birds, and the whippoorwills cry all night. The whippoorwills also dust themselves in the sand roads, and when they are approached at night their eyes blaze red. Nighthawks dive in the evening, and when they come out of the dive their wings open and make an explosive sound, like a sonic boom. Great-crested fly-catchers hang snakeskins outside their holes in hollow pines. Eighty-four different kinds of birds breed in the Pine Barrens, not to mention the ones that make stop-overs there, and the natives include Cooper's hawks, alder flycatchers, brown creepers, Henslow's sparrows, red crossbills, Baltimore orioles, green herons, black ducks, yellow-billed cuckoos, sharp-shinned hawks, great horned owls, screech owls, bobwhites, woodcocks, ruby-throated hummingbirds, white-breasted nuthatches, indigo buntings, scarlet tanagers, brown-headed cowbirds, Carolina chickadees, bluebirds, blue jays, brown thrashers, turkey vultures, meadowlarks, yellow-breasted chats, hooded warblers, prairie warblers, pine warblers, yellow warblers, chestnut-sided warblers, blue-winged warblers, black-and-white warblers, parula warblers, prothonotary warblers, red-eyed vireos, white-eyed vireos, cedar waxwings, Carolina wrens, catbirds, and robins. The most common bird in the Pine Barrens is the towhee. When a man from the National Park Service asked a state forester, "What is your biggest bird, your most dramatic bird?," the forester answered, "I would say the bald eagle."

Ducks make their skid-in landings on Pine Barrens rivers and swim along alertly, heads high, looking out for themselves, when suddenly and involuntarily they disappear beneath the surface. "Snappers lie under the water and wait for ducks," Fred Brown said one day when he and I and Bill Wasovwich had gone out for a drive in the pines. "The snappers grabs the ducks by the feet and pulls them right under there, and in two or three minutes they drown and the snappers eats them. The snappers catch big ducks." Snapping turtles in the Pine Barrens are sometimes a foot and a half long and almost as wide. They weigh fifty pounds. Pineys trap them in fykes, and fry their delicious white meat. Minks and muskrats are also trapped, for their pelts.

Beaver dams are frequent in the pines. Beaver lakes attract ducks and encourage expansion in the communities of pickerel, muskrats, minks, and otters. The beavers are big and surprisingly fierce.

"I don't believe there's an animal in these woods could take on a beaver," Bill said.

Fred seemed to disagree. "A fish otter is a fighter," he said. "A fish otter can kill a dog."

Some of the pickerel are more than three feet long. It is said that people used to drift down the rivers and catch thirty or forty in a morning. The pickerel are not quite that plentiful anymore. With catfish, they are the only large fresh-water fish in the rivers. The acid content of the water is too high for trout. In addition to green frogs, sphagnum frogs, leopard frogs, and swamp-chorus frogs, there is a tree frog in the pines that has considerable status. This is *Hyla andersoni*, Anderson's tree frog, a rare creature prized by naturalists and found almost nowhere else. Anderson's tree frogs live in the Pine Barrens in abundance. They are only one and three-eighths inches long with their legs stretched out. At night, they go *wonk, wonk, wonk*, and the art of stalking them is to follow the sound and, at the key moment, surprise them with light. This is not simple, because the frogs are ventriloquists. But they are worth seeing, for their skins are a brilliant green, trimmed with white, and they have lavender stripes down the sides of their legs. They look like state troopers. The rattlesnake community is small in the Pine Barrens, and consists wholly of timber rattlesnakes. It is said to be centered at Mt.

Misery. A man known as Rattlesnake Ace Pittman once lived in that area. He made his living collecting rattlesnakes for zoos and shoe manufacturers. There are puff adders in the pines, and beautiful corn snakes, five feet long, with red eyes, red tongues, and red bodies. While I was riding along one of the sand roads with the three men from the National Park Service, we came upon a mottled brown-and-white snake that was more than six feet long and about two inches in diameter. The Park Service men jumped out of the car, and one of them set up a tripod and began to photograph the snake while another, using a snake stick, played with it. The snake coiled. It raised its forward third in an S curve, as if preparing to strike, and it took an enormous breath that filled its body with air from one end to the other and swelled it to the diameter of a fire hose. Then it exhaled with a sensational hiss, so loud and menacing that everyone jumped backward. With the hiss came a rattling sound. The snake was really furious. None of the men from the Park Service knew what kind of snake it was, although at the time we were on the southwestern slope of Bear Swamp Hill, in the middle of the Pine Barrens, and it was a pine snake.

The gray fox climbs like a cat. He goes up leaning cedars. He hides in the forks of oaks. In the daytime, he sometimes sleeps in a crow's nest. Red foxes are rare in the pines. It is the gray fox that the native hunters hunt. The hunters follow their hounds in pickup trucks. "I used to have the best dogs that you ever heard run in the woods," Fred Brown once told me. "American

foxhounds. I never had no big packs of twelve or fifteen, like some people. I had six, or four, sometimes
only two." A mother foxhound can listen to her puppies
hunting and by the sound of their cries she can tell what
they are after. If the puppies are chasing a rabbit, she
doesn't move. If they have smelled a fox, she gets up and
joins them. She will not go after deer. Deer are a nuis-
ance to foxhunters, and their good dogs are, as they put
it, deer-broke. For a hunt, several packs are brought together, since one object of the sport is to see who has
the best dogs. Experienced hounds know how to "cold-
trail," and they are turned loose first, while the younger
hounds stay in the backs of the pickup trucks. Three or
four cold-trailing dogs move around for a while, and
soon, as the trail becomes hot, their voices change. What
began as a long, drawling bay becomes shorter and
shorter as the scent grows stronger, until the sound of
the hounds becomes what the hunters call a chop. The
chop intensifies, and when it reaches a certain pitch
and tempo the hunters know that the hounds are about
to "jump a fox"—the moment when the chase begins.
The younger hounds are released, and off goes the pack
through the woods, while the men in pickup trucks race
up and down the sand roads, frequently stopping to
listen, then gunning flat out in the shifting direction of
the sound. The idea is to anticipate where the fox and
the pack are going, get there first, and catch sight of the
fox as he crosses a sand road. The man who scores
the most sightings has proved himself to be the most skillful hunter, so there is a great deal of lying about who

saw the fox how many times. A good, and lucky, hunter might see the fox three times in a four-hour chase. When the fox is sighted, a point of even greater importance is: Whose dog is first on the fox's trail? There is a great deal of lying about that, too. A strung-out pack can spoil a chase, since concentrated sound is essential to the hunters, and when the dogs "pack up" on a fox the ideal is that they run so close together that a blanket thrown over them would cover them all. The hunters' wives ask their husbands why they go to so much effort just to hear a pack of dogs bark, and the hunters say that it is not barking they hear but music. They say that the sound of a pack of hounds is as musical as the sound of a flight of wild geese. Each dog apparently yells in a different key. The hunters also say that they learn more from foxes than foxes learn from them. The fox handles the day. The fox knows the age and experience of the dogs that are chasing him. The fox maintains his lead position in the chase, but if the dogs are slow and inept he himself slows down and keeps things interesting for the hunters. The chase finally ends when the fox is treed. None of the foxhunters of the Pine Barrens would dream of killing such a creature. One of them climbs the tree with a bag and, as gently as possible, puts the fox inside. The fox is then driven to a place in the woods that is safe and distant from the hounds. The bag is opened and he jumps out.

In Atlantic City not long ago, a man bit into a hamburger and found that it was full of buckshot. He was really eating a venisonburger, and the meat had come from the Pine Barrens, where deer poaching has been going on for exactly as many years as there have been fish-and-game laws. One day when I stopped in to see a family I know in Washington Township, the woman of the house excused herself at one point and made a phone call, and she said to the person who answered, "Charlie, do you know where I can get some deer meat now? Is Butch poaching? He's in jail? Is Petrosch poaching? No? Well, you think it over overnight. The meat's O.K., right? No ticks? No worms? O.K., you think it over." This was in August, and she explained to me that from the middle of May until about the first of August deer have ticks under their skins, which heavily spot the meat. "And you can get fevers," she said. "I know. I've had them." The kind of order she was placing was for small-scale poaching, for home consumption, and it was a negotiation between one piney and another. "I don't call it poaching when you're putting meat on the table," the woman went on. Most people in the Pine Barrens would agree with her. They know that it is against the law to kill deer out of season—the shooting season is six days long and comes in December—but they seem to feel that the law was made to control sportsmen hunters, and not to deny a native right to the people of the woods. Market hunting, as they call commercial poaching, is something else. The state police told me of one deerjacker who used to kill over three hundred deer a year. Deerjackers are not all pineys. Some are from towns outside the Pine Barrens. One, who was arrested a short time ago, was a city youth from Philadelphia.

When a deerjacker goes out poaching, the first thing he does is to stop at one of several gin mills on Route 206, which runs north and south through the western part of the pines. There he meets a contact man. Over beers, the two discuss current prices. Carcasses have been bringing about twenty-five dollars in recent years. Then the poacher leaves. It is night, and he moves into the woods in his automobile on the sand roads. He has with him a hand spotlight that plugs into the car's cigarette lighter. A permanent, mounted spotlight would be too much of a signal to police. He also has a 30-30 rifle or a shotgun. He drives, as often as not, to a deer-diversionary strip, where he stops his car and waits. Deer-diversionary strips are swaths in the pines, miles long and only a few yards wide, where crops such as soybeans and lespedeza are planted by the state so that deer will eat there and do less damage to blueberry fields and cranberry bogs, and to farm crops on the periphery of the woods. A bit unintelligently, the state put these diversionary strips beside sand roads, thus establishing some of the world's most convenient poaching grounds. If the strips had been cleared even a few hundred yards from the roads, the annual kill by poachers would be much smaller. Fish-and-game men say that modern poachers, for the most part, will not go after deer if they have to walk. When a poacher has made his kill, or kills, he goes back to the gin mill and has another drink with the contact man. They go outside and exchange the meat for the money. Then the poacher goes back inside, as often as not, and drinks up more of his profit.

Last year, in Toms River, which is just outside the Pine Barrens, Fred Brown went into a short-order restaurant and ordered a hamburger. When it came and he had taken a bite of it, he said to the man behind the counter, "That hamburger wasn't raised on corn."

"What *was* it raised on?" the man said.

"Acorns."

"Keep quiet," the man said, and he gave Fred a second deerburger on the house.

"The second one was deer and pork mixed," Fred told me. "And that is good. Hell, yes."

Pineys have a curious regard for the New Jersey state law that forbids hunting with rifles. They generally use shotguns, like the thousands of hunters who come into the pines in hunting season, but they sometimes perform alterations that turn the shotguns at least partway into rifles. Fred once took a ball bearing from a pump engine, "crimped" it into a brass shotgun shell, and killed a deer. Some men string buckshot together with wire, after drilling holes in the shot, so that the connected pellets will carry farther and stay close together, like the flying chains of cannon days. All over the woods, gun clubs have cabins, full of cots, for men who spend one week in the pines each year. The legitimate deer kill is large there. More deer are harvested in Washington Township than in any other township in New Jersey, and New Jersey as a whole is among the best deer-hunting states in the country. There are more deer

§ 142 §

per square mile in the woods of New Jersey than there are in the woods of Maine. An American Indian from Kingston, New Jersey, goes into the pines every fall and hunts deer the way his forebears did. He waits in a tree until a deer passes beneath, then he drops on it with a knife in his hand and slits its throat. Few among the autumn throng are in that kind of shape. They walk for miles and miles, eat too much, drink too much, and frequently suffer heart attacks. The state police used to keep a jeep on patrol just to remove heart-attack patients from the woods. "They eat so heavy it's just too much for their body," one trooper told me. "They want to be woodsmen one week of the year." For every man who has a heart attack, fifty get lost. The forest perspectives are so deceptive that even the natives get lost, but they at least know what to do. Charlie Leek told me, "If I'm lost, I sit right down. A piney gets lost, he'll sit down. You take your native who lives around here, he'll sit, and he'll think. On the south side of the tree you find the longest branches. Most all your streams here runs north and south. On a clear day, you've got your sun. The worst I've ever been lost was over near Atsion. They got a fern bush over there high as your head. Everything looks the same. I been lost in the Plains, too. Deer play games with hunters there. The Plains are not like the big woods, where it's more open between the trees. Deer walk right by you in the Plains, ten feet away. In the Plains, they can hide from you, don't you think that they can't."

The director of New Jersey's Fish and Game Division,

Lester MacNamara, was born and grew up in the San Joaquin Valley of California. He went to the University of California, and after that, in 1929, to the Game Conservation Institute in Clinton, New Jersey, a school that no longer exists. He is a big, soft-spoken man with a splendidly weatherworn face. Before reaching his present position, he wandered the state for years as chief of the Bureau of Wildlife. "When I left California, I thought I was coming to a place that would be just one line of houses," he once told me. "I found it entirely different. New Jersey has always been very interesting to me, not only from the point of view of wildlife but of its wilderness, too. I went back to California in 1950. Places I used to hunt when I was a kid, you couldn't hunt. I hurried back here. The Fish and Game Division has purchased a lot of land down in the Pine Barrens. I hate to think of losing the pines to industry."

9

Vision

IN EVERY DECADE FOR MORE THAN A CEN-
tury, there have been men of vision who could see, and
somehow could make others see, urban skylines in the
pines—with beautiful, pine-scented subdivisions set close
to throbbing factories. Roughly five hundred major
real-estate promotions based on these intracranial pan-
oramas have been set in motion since 1850, and the selling points have always been irresistible. After all, industry once prospered in the pines. It could prosper
again. No matter what a buyer pays per acre, the land
values seem certain to rise, and the purchase of land is
an excellent speculative investment. The long succession
of instant paradises has made the Pine Barrens the scene
of what is perhaps the country's only permanent non-
existent land boom. In the eighteen-sixties, the name
of Atsion was changed to Fruitland and the surrounding
woods were divided into small lots. Pamphlets titled
"Cheap Lands, Homes for the Homeless, the Wild Lands
of New Jersey" were handed out on New York City
sidewalks. "The New Jersey wilderness shall be trans-

formed into farms and fields of grain," the pamphlets said. "A large population should take the place of a few scattered families of woodchoppers and coal-burners and their concomitants of ignorance, sin, and wretchedness. Let all this forest be made flagrant with fruit blossoms!" In a short time, the name of Fruitland was changed back to Atsion, and the woods remained unflagrant. A New York doctor once started a clinic on Apple Pie Hill. He bottled and sold water from a spring, and he divided the slopes into five-acre lots and sold them, too. Almost nothing was built, and the only structure there now is the fire tower. A mile or so west of Apple Pie Hill was Paisley, the Magic City. Paisley was an instant Athens, where, according to advertisements that ran in the New York *World* in 1889, "Your neighbors are great artists, authors, composers, medical men, lawyers." Wavering buyers were warned against delay: "Grasp this last opportunity. We will never sell lots in Paisley at these prices again." The Magic City covered fourteen hundred acres and included thirteen thousand lots. The promoters bought the land for three dollars and sixty-seven cents an acre and sold it, usually, for three hundred and seventy-five dollars an acre, although to get things moving they gave lots away. There were Paisley offices in New York, Philadelphia, Washington, and Chicago. More than three thousand people bought Paisley land, and nearly all of them, in expectation of turnover profits, sat back and waited for the others to build. The nutrient-free soils of Paisley were advertised as "the finest farmland in central New

Jersey," and the town itself was described as "a manu-facturing center with an academy of music, conserva-tories, schools, and colleges." At Paisley's peak of de-velopment, in 1890, the Magic City consisted of twelve wooden buildings. Nothing is there now but a stucco gun club that was built in recent times. Over the years, more than a million people have bought or otherwise acquired lots in the Pine Barrens on which no houses have ever been built. There were once twenty-two thousand proposed houses on proposed roads in Bass River Township alone. The lots were twenty feet wide and eighty feet deep, or roughly the size of a brown-stone lot in Manhattan. Prosperity Park, outside Chats-worth, consisted of eighteen thousand lots, twenty-five by a hundred feet. In the nineteen-twenties, lots were given away as premiums with new subscriptions to a Philadelphia newspaper. In the Depression, deeds to lots in the Pine Barrens were given away as door prizes at movie theatres and to purchasers of encyclopedias. The selling price at the time was five dollars a lot. When prospective buyers actually came to see the land, pro-moters tied pears and apples to the limbs of pine trees and stationed fishermen in small boats in Pine Barrens lakes with dead pickerel on the ends of their lines and instructions to pull the fish out of the water every ten minutes. The typical development never existed on any-thing but paper. Some subdivisions were cleared but never built, and the vegetation soon moved back in to cover almost all the evidence. In one lonely place in the woods today is a street sign marked Fifth Avenue.

In many areas of the Pine Barrens, titles are so cloudy —as a result of all the speculation—that about twelve thousand acres of the woods are virtually a no man's land. Modern real-estate sharks have further complicated the situation by faking the signatures of "original owners" in order to gain title to pieces of land. It has been said of one such realtor that he is able to disappear into empty woods and emerge moments later with a signed deed. When four thousand four hundred acres of land were offered for sale a few years ago, the state looked into the property and found that the would-be sellers owned only twelve hundred acres. In other places, the land-ownership picture is clearer. There are two hundred and fifty square miles of state forest in the central Pine Barrens, in areas that are not contiguous. The Plains are, for the most part, privately owned, and so are all the woods for several miles around Chatsworth in every direction. More than half the private land is in absentee ownership. Speculators think no less of the pines now than they did in the days of the Magic City. They are just a little quieter about it. They are waiting. The Pine Barrens were bypassed by the farmers of the seventeenth century, but they are unlikely to be bypassed now. The simple facts of all that space and all that subsurface water increase in importance with each new nail that goes into the megalopolis of which the Pine Barrens are the geographical center. Many private owners have more than a thousand acres, and a number of corporations have been organized for the purpose of real-estate speculation in the pines. One man in North

§ 148 §

Jersey owns five thousand acres near Chatsworth and wants to turn them into an industrial park. There are individual holdings in the same area of four thousand acres, two thousand acres, and fifty-five hundred acres. The Rutherford Stuyvesant estate, known as the Lacey Tract, contains fourteen thousand five hundred acres in the northeastern pines and is owned now by a syndicate. A nine-thousand-acre property nearby is owned by another syndicate. Pineland sells, on the average, for a hundred and fifty dollars an acre. There is a sign on a tree on Carranza's Road that says "2,150 Acres—For Information Call New York City, TRafalgar 3-9111." Some people in the pines say that they wouldn't mind seeing industry come in, since they could use the tax money. Others have refused to sell land even for small roadside refreshment stands, because of the changes such things effect in the nature of the woods.

Of all the schemes that have ever been created for the development of the Pine Barrens, the most exhaustive and expensive one is the proposal for a jetport and a new city. Under this plan, a spur of the Garden State Parkway would take off into the woods from Toms River, soon passing beneath the central business district of a city of two hundred and fifty thousand people. Beyond the city, the road would go through a green belt, then through an industrial park, and then under the runways and past the terminal building of the largest airport on earth—four times as large as Newark Airport, LaGuardia, and Kennedy put together. As a supersonic jetport, it would serve a third of the United States, and supersonic jets would land there ninety minutes after leaving Paris. Shuttle jets would fly passengers to inland airports, and hundred-and-fifty-mile-an-hour trains would take travellers to Philadelphia in twenty minutes and to New York in thirty. All this was worked out by Herbert H. Smith Associates, of Trenton, under contract to the Pinelands Regional Planning Board, a group consisting of representatives of Burlington and Ocean Counties. The study cost a hundred and twenty thousand dollars and was largely paid for by the federal government. It was published in 1964, and since then it has been drawing abuse from conservationists, hunters, campers, and pineys—along with studious disregard from the Port of New York Authority. The Federal Aviation Administration has said that the jetport would interfere with present air-traffic patterns but that if the state wanted to build it F.A.A. approval could be secured. The New Jersey legislature has displayed some interest in the project, and the governor has appointed a committee of businessmen to study the feasibility of a jetport in the pines.

Forked River Mountain, in the Lacey Tract, is in the center of the proposed city. With Herbert Smith, the planner, I went up there one morning to have a look at the site. It was a clear summer day, with big clouds in the sky and a cool wind blowing. The view from the top of the hill was spacious, and unbroken pineland reached away for miles, streaked with dark lines of cedars. "I hope I don't start to cry," Smith said. "This is a planner's dream. From this elevation, we could move right out

§ 150 §

onto the central-business-district platform—two hundred and forty acres of stores and plazas and high buildings in the middle of the city, for pedestrians only. The parkway goes under the platform, and there is parking space down there for twenty thousand cars. Battery-operated taxis and battery-operated scooters are permitted on the platform. The sidewalks move, too. Even outside the platform, underpasses and bridges make it possible for you to walk from any part of the city to any other part without crossing a street. This area of the pinelands simply begins to jump out at you if you're going to go for urbanization. It's magnificent. It's just magnificent. I can see those goldarn structures now, surrounded with green."

Smith is a trim, likable, red-headed man in his forties. He comes from Mayfield, Kentucky. He was educated at the University of Cincinnati, got an M.A. in planning from Cornell, and worked in the planning office of the State of New Jersey before setting up his own practice. In my car, we drove a short distance to a dry, flat area that had been badly burned not long before. The spiky remains of the trees were grotesque. Smith remarked that we were in the middle of the campus of the city college. As we drove on, along a sand road, he said, "We've come through the city college into the high-density low-income housing area." The car was bumping over a corduroy surface of cedar logs, but I imagined myself cruising along Avenue D on the lower East Side of Manhattan. A burned-up 1949 Chrysler, which had been abandoned in the high-density low-income housing area of the proposed city, was sieved with bullet holes and had ninety-three bullet holes in the driver's door alone. "There are two elementary schools nearby," Smith said, studying a map on his knees. "Now we are in a neighborhood of town houses and garden apartments. . . . Now we are just about to pass over the Garden State Parkway connection. We are between a high-rise area and the city-center core. . . . Now we're in the middle of the lake—twenty feet deep, two miles long. That's the country club over there. . . . Now we're right in the middle of the hoity-toity housing." In the middle of the hoity-toity housing was the only building we had seen in two hours of driving around the city. It was made of purplish-tan bricks and had a corrugated roof, and its name was over the door—Ironside Gun Club.

Smith sees his plan as "a happy marriage between conservation and economic development," since—in concert with the new city, the jetport, and the industrial park—it calls for five hundred square miles of state forest, or twice the amount of state forest that is now set aside in the pines. He believes that no unilateral conservation plan could accomplish as much. He suggests also that a possible alternative to the new city would be three new towns with populations of about eighty thousand each. "What we're pleading for is that a pinelands area be defined and then developed according to a single, controlled plan," he said. "It goes against my political philosophy, but sovereign government can do it, and I don't know of another area where both economic and conservation potential can be realized so completely. In this situation right here, we have the epitome of the problem of planning in a democratic society. We can make the plan, but then we run into conflict with all the people who want to profit from the land by exploitation. Private enterprise *could* do a hell of a lot. If, say, Esso and Portland Cement and Johns-Manville saw the potential, a development corporation could be formed and the new city could be developed by free enterprise. Private enterprise needs to prove that it can do this. Or the state could create a Pinelands Development Authority, with the right of eminent domain and the right to sell bonds with state credit pledged behind them. This is the way the Garden State Parkway Authority was set up. To do this, you have to declare a public purpose—in this case, water potential, conservation of an open area, and a new city with a decent way of life for people in a region that has economic potential. Planning has to be statewide for the pines. Otherwise, you have local planning boards coming up with controlled hodgepodge. I will predict that if nothing at all is done in terms of planned development here, within twenty years the area will be so spotted with exploitative development that it will be impossible to assemble the land into something that is sensibly planned. The state has about five years in which to act."

We moved on to see the site of the jetport, which would cover thirty-two thousand five hundred acres and would eliminate virtually all of the Upper and Lower Plains, several ponds, a lake, an entire state forest, and

Bear Swamp Hill. The dual runways, forming a great square, would each be two miles wide. The over-all cleared area for each runway—including overrun areas at the ends—would be five miles long. "You get a hell of a lot less fog here than you do at the New York airports," Smith said. "This one would be open fifty per cent more than Newark, Kennedy, and LaGuardia." We were standing on the observation platform of the fire tower on Bear Swamp Hill. The ranger, in the cabin above us, was listening to rock 'n' roll. Looking out over the immense forest, Smith went on to say, "One of our problems is that you can't get people to believe that this area is as big as this. They can't believe that you could come down here and build a fifty-one-square-mile airport and not have a structure problem—not even one building visible from here to the horizon. Bear Swamp Hill is in the terminal-service area, where the planes would come in and unload. I can just see those supersonic transports coming in here now. Gorgeous! And when they take off, you can get them out over the ocean before they break the sound barrier. Here comes Flight 424, which left London one and a half hours ago. Brisbane is five hours away."

Many people would like to see the conservation part of Smith's plan developed wholly on its own. A group called the Pine Barrens Conservationists has advanced a proposal that ninety thousand acres—including all of the Plains—be preserved under the administration of the National Park Service. The area would be called a national reserve, would lie between existing state forests,

including the Wharton Forest, and would effectively
keep one big segment of the central pines perpetually
wild. The New Jersey Audubon Society has a proposal
for a national monument that encompasses even more
land. In a general way, the National Park Service has
offered encouragement to these plans, but some of the
Park Service people I talked with seemed to think that
the state should preserve the Pine Barrens. They pointed
out that the laws are uncompromising under which various federal preserves are established, and that making
even a part of the woods a national domain might limit
too severely the uses to which the land could be put.
State people, for their part, said frankly that no land
is safe in the hands of the state. New Jersey's Forest
Park Reservation Act is among the most elastic conservation laws ever written. The state can use its forest
land for any purpose it chooses. There is no guarantee
that state forests will be preserved. In 1951, a small state
park was sold outright to Western Union. In 1961, a
large piece of a state forest, including a section of the
Appalachian Trail, was sold to the New Jersey Power
& Light Co. On the other hand, federal law would pro-
hibit the removal of subsurface water from a Pine Barrens national monument, no matter how badly it was
needed. Controlled burning would be forbidden, and so
would hunting, although ecologists who have studied
the Pine Barrens feel that the deer count has to be kept
down or the balance of nature will be seriously upset.
In a Pine Barrens national park, these limitations would
be identical. Calling the area a national reserve might

solve the problem. Another alternative might be a national recreation area, but when this is mentioned National Park Service people say that new lakes would have to be made, big enough for powerboats; cabins, tent-platform cities, and even airfields would have to be built. "You can't make a national recreation area just for a few people who have canoes," one man told me. "People who go to a national recreation area want to play in the water and drink beer and eat hot dogs and that sort of deal. Orchids? Eagles? If they happen to be there, O.K.—but they have to be there along with the other things. The Pine Barrens probably should be state-managed."

Given the futilities of that debate, given the sort of attention that is ordinarily paid to plans put forward by conservationists, and given the great numbers and the crossed purposes of all the big and little powers that would have to work together to accomplish *anything* on a major scale in the pines, it would appear that the Pine Barrens are not very likely to be the subject of dramatic decrees or acts of legislation. They seem to be headed slowly toward extinction. In retrospect, people may one day look back upon the final stages of the development of the great unbroken Eastern city and be able to say at what moment all remaining undeveloped land should have been considered no longer a potential asset to individuals but an asset of the society at large—perhaps a social necessity. Meanwhile, up goes a sign—"Whispering Pines, Two and Three Bedrooms, $11,900"—and down go seventy-five acres of trees. Up goes another sign: "Industry!! Jackson Township Has an Abundance of Water!.," and another: "Dreamwood Acres, from $13,900," and another: "Deer Hollow Estates, Five Models," and another: "Sav-Cote, Inc., Manufacturers of Liquid Plastic Coatings," and others: "Buck's Outlet Store," "Pine Tree Inn—Dinners, Snacks, Package Goods," "A. G. Weller, Landscaping, Bulldozing," "Will Build to Suit." At the rate of a few hundred yards or even a mile or so each year, the perimeter of the pines contracts.

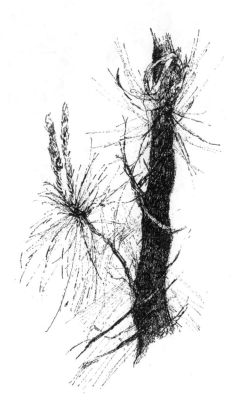